Copyright

The moral right of N.R. Smith to be identifi[...] [...]rted by him in accordance with the Cop[...]

ISBN-13: 9[...]
ISBN-10: [...]

Some content included within this publication has been kindly reproduced from Wikipedia as indicated in the attributions of specific images or end notes. Consequently the parts of this work taken from Wikipedia are licensed under the Creative Commons Attribution-ShareAlike 4.0 International License.
All other content is Copyright © N.R. Smith 2017.
To view a copy of this license visit https://creativecommons.org/licenses/by-sa/4.0/

A catalogue record for this book is available from the British Library, the U.S. Copyright Office, and the Canadian Intellectual Property Office.

Disclaimer

Although every effort has been made to provide complete and accurate information, there are no warranties, expressed or implied, or representations as to the accuracy of content in this book. No liability or responsibility for any error or omissions in the information contained in this book is assumed.

Contents

Introduction 3

1960 5
1961 13
1962 20
1963 28
1964 35
1965 44
1966 53
1967 62
1968 73
1969 81

Alphabetical listing by artist 90
Alphbetical listing by title 136

References 181

Hello folks and welcome to British Top 20 Hits of the 1960's.

I'm a music collector and I've collected many of the publications that have been generated on the subject. What I found however, was a lack of easy to read information on the subject of just top 20 chart hits. With this in mind I set about producing just that - an easy to read, practical listing of every British top 20 single from 1960 to 1969.

There are many excellent publications that can provide you with all kinds of details concerning the date that a particular single first entered the UK chart, the label it was released on, the catalogue number etc., and I don't believe that I would have added any value to you by repeating that information here. On the contrary, rather than repeat what is already available I've tried to provide something which is not, and that is a clear listing of every single artist and title that occupied a top 20 position in the British chart in a particular year, the highest position that the single reached in that year, and the week ending (W/E) date of the chart in which that position was reached. As you read through the charts you'll see that the information has been laid out in chronological chart-date order, starting with January and moving on through to December. You should note that there are a small number of occasions when you will not find any chart movements listed for the last week of the year. **This is not an error** - the reason is simply because there were no chart movements listed in the last chart of the year and therefore all entries remained in their previous positions as shown in the chart of the previous week.

In addition to the chart information that has been compiled by year, and to make life easier for you, I've added an **alphabetical list by artist** of every top 20 hit for the decade, and an **alphabetical list by title** of every top 20 hit for the decade. Finally, I've tried to provide you with a flavour of each of the years by including a little light-hearted trivia on some of the events of the day.

I do hope that you derive as much knowledge and entertainment from the finished article as I did putting it all together!

                    For details of other books available in this series please visit
                                www.BritishTop20Hits.com

Enjoy………..

Nick

Thanks & acknowledgements

With sincere thanks to Natalia, Gregory and Andrew for your patience and understanding.

Who knows, you guys might even find this useful one day! ☺

My love to you all

1960

Welcome to the lighter side of life in Britain in 1960

The music ……

Artist	Title	Highest position this year	W/E date
Max Bygraves	Jingle bell rock	7	07-Jan
Beverley Sisters	Little donkey	16	07-Jan
Bobby Darin	Mack the Knife	19	07-Jan
Russ Conway	More and more party pops	11	07-Jan
Winifred Atwell	Piano party	15	07-Jan
Paul Anka	Put your head on my shoulder	17	07-Jan
Frankie Laine	Rawhide	6	07-Jan
Avons	Seven little girls (sitting in the back seat)	3	07-Jan
Russ Conway	Snow coach	8	07-Jan
Cliff Richard & The Shadows	Travellin' light	5	07-Jan
Emile Ford & The Checkmates	What do you want to make those eyes at me for?	1	07-Jan
Adam Faith	What do you want?	2	07-Jan
Connie Francis	Among my souvenirs	11	14-Jan
Marty Wilde	Bad boy	7	14-Jan
Tommy Steele	Little white bull	6	14-Jan
Neil Sedaka	Oh Carol	3	14-Jan
Johnny & The Hurricanes	Red River rock	10	14-Jan
Duane Eddy	Some kind-a-earthquake	12	14-Jan
Sandy Nelson	Teen beat	18	14-Jan
Johnny & The Hurricanes	Reveille rock	14	21-Jan

Artist	Title	#	Date
Fats Domino	Be my guest	11	21-Jan
Elmer Bernstein	Staccato's theme	4	21-Jan
Little Tony	Too good	19	21-Jan
Drifters	Dance with me	17	28-Jan
Frankie Avalon	Why	20	28-Jan
Ernie Fields & His Orchestra	In the mood	13	04-Feb
Michael Holliday	Starry eyed	1	04-Feb
Cliff Richard & The Shadows	Expresso bongo - EP (Love / A voice in the wilderness / The shrine on the second floor / Bongo blues (the Shadows)	14	11-Feb
Guy Mitchell	Heartaches by the number	5	11-Feb
Cliff Richard & The Shadows	Voice in the wilderness	2	11-Feb
Anthony Newley	Why	1	11-Feb
Marty Robbins	El Paso	19	18-Feb
Bobby Darin	La mer (Beyond the sea)	8	18-Feb
Johnny Mathis	Misty	12	18-Feb
Freddy Cannon	Way down yonder in New Orleans	3	18-Feb
Platters	Harbour lights	11	03-Mar
Craig Douglas	Pretty blue eyes	4	03-Mar
Duane Eddy	Bonnie came back	12	09-Mar
Adam Faith	Poor me	1	09-Mar
Jerry Lordan	Who could be bluer?	16	09-Mar
Emile Ford & The Checkmates	On a slow boat to China	3	16-Mar
Russ Conway	Royal event	15	16-Mar
Mr. Acker Bilk & His Paramount Jazz Band	Summer set	5	16-Mar
Marv Johnson	You got what it takes	7	16-Mar
Lance Fortune	Be mine	4	23-Mar
Perry Como	Delaware	3	23-Mar
Everly Brothers	Let it be me	13	23-Mar
Gene Vincent	My heart	16	23-Mar
Johnny Preston	Running bear	1	23-Mar
Billy Fury	Collette	9	30-Mar

Artist	Title		Date
Bobby Rydell	Wild one	7	30-Mar
Percy Faith	Theme from 'A Summer Place'	2	30-Mar
Lonnie Donegan	My old man's a dustman	1	06-Apr
Jack Scott	What in the world's come over you?	11	13-Apr
Johnny & The Hurricanes	Beatnik fly	8	20-Apr
Fats Domino	Country boy	19	20-Apr
Cliff Richard & The Shadows	Easily fall in love with you	2	20-Apr
Max Bygraves	Fings ain't wot they used to be	5	20-Apr
Jimmy Jones	Handy man	3	20-Apr
Bryan Johnson	Looking high, high, high	20	20-Apr
Bobby Darin	Clementine	8	27-Apr
John Barry Seven	Hit and miss	10	27-Apr
Elvis Presley	Stuck on you	3	27-Apr
Anthony Newley	Do you mind?	1	04-May
Everly Brothers	Cathy's clown	1	11-May
King Brothers	Standing on the corner	4	11-May
Ella Fitzgerald	Mack the Knife	19	25-May
Adam Faith	Someone else's baby	2	25-May
Johnny Preston	Cradle of love	2	01-Jun
Steve Lawrence	Footsteps	4	01-Jun
Craig Douglas	The heart of a teenage girl	10	01-Jun
Brenda Lee	Sweet nothin's	4	08-Jun
Russ Conway	Lucky five	14	15-Jun
Duane Eddy	Shazam	4	15-Jun
Emile Ford & The Checkmates	You'll never know what you're missing	12	15-Jun
Freddy Cannon	The urge	18	15-Jun
Neil Sedaka	Stairway to heaven	8	22-Jun
Jim Reeves	He'll have to go	12	29-Jun
Lonnie Donegan	I wanna go home	5	29-Jun
Billy Bland	Let the little girl dance	15	29-Jun
Connie Francis	Mama / Robot man	2	29-Jun

Nat 'King' Cole	That's you	10	29-Jun
Eddie Cochran	Three steps to heaven	1	29-Jun
Billy Fury	That's love	19	06-Jul
Johnny & The Hurricanes	Down yonder	8	13-Jul
Jimmy Jones	Good timin'	1	13-Jul
Tommy Steele	What a mouth	5	13-Jul
Michael Cox	Angela Jones	7	20-Jul
Gene Vincent	Pistol packin' mama	15	20-Jul
Frank Sinatra	River, stay 'way from my door	18	20-Jul
Connie Stevens	Sixteen reasons	9	20-Jul
Tommy Bruce & The Bruisers	Ain't misbehavin'	3	27-Jul
Adam Faith	When Johnny comes marching home / Made you	5	27-Jul
Anthony Newley	If she should come to you	4	03-Aug
Gary Mills	Look for a star	7	03-Aug
Cliff Richard	Please don't tease	1	03-Aug
Johnny Kidd & The Pirates	Shakin' all over	1	10-Aug
Brian Hyland	Itsy bitsy teeny weeny yellow polka dot bikini	8	17-Aug
Brenda Lee	I'm sorry	12	24-Aug
Rolf Harris	Tie me kangaroo down	9	24-Aug
Shadows	Apache	1	31-Aug
Ken Dodd	Love is like a violin	8	31-Aug
King Brothers	Mais oui	16	31-Aug
Everly Brothers	When will I be loved	4	31-Aug
Johnny Preston	Feel so fine	18	07-Sep
Fats Domino	Walking to New Orleans	19	07-Sep
Duane Eddy	Because they're young	2	14-Sep
Lonnie Donegan	Lorelei	10	14-Sep
Kaye Sisters	Paper roses	7	14-Sep
Elvis Presley	A mess of blues	2	21-Sep

Artist	Title	Weeks	Date
Connie Francis	Everybody's somebody's fool	5	21-Sep
Mark Wynter	Image of a girl	11	28-Sep
Ricky Valance	Tell Laura I love her	1	05-Oct
Cliff Richard	Nine times out of ten	3	12-Oct
Ventures	Walk don't run	8	12-Oct
Adam Faith	How about that!	4	19-Oct
Russ Conway	Passing breeze	16	19-Oct
Hank Locklin	Please help me I'm falling	9	19-Oct
Everly Brothers	Lucille / So sad	4	26-Oct
Frank Sinatra	Nice 'n' easy	15	26-Oct
Roy Orbison	Only the lonely	1	26-Oct
John Barry Seven	Walk don't run	11	26-Oct
Shirley Bassey	As long as he needs me	2	02-Nov
Sam Cooke	Chain gang	9	02-Nov
Bob Luman	Let's think about livin'	6	02-Nov
Elvis Presley	It's now or never	1	09-Nov
Viscounts	Shortnin' bread	16	09-Nov
Johnny Burnette	Dreamin'	5	16-Nov
Piltdown Men	MacDonald's cave	14	16-Nov
Johnny Mathis	My love for you	9	16-Nov
Emile Ford & The Checkmates	Them there eyes	18	16-Nov
Johnny & The Hurricanes	Rocking goose	3	23-Nov
Nat 'King' Cole	Just as much as ever	18	30-Nov
Duane Eddy	Kommotion	13	30-Nov
Charlie Drake	Mr. Custer	12	30-Nov
Connie Francis	My heart has a mind of it's own	3	30-Nov
Peter Sellers & Sophia Loren	Goodness gracious me	4	07-Dec
Shadows	Man of mystery / The stranger	5	07-Dec
Drifters	Save the last dance for me	2	07-Dec
Nina & Frederick	Little donkey	3	14-Dec
Lonnie Donegan	Lively	13	14-Dec
Frank Sinatra	Ol' MacDonald	11	14-Dec

Anthony Newley	Strawberry fair	3	21-Dec
Roy Orbison	Blue angel	11	28-Dec
Emile Ford & The Checkmates	Counting teardrops	20	28-Dec
Max Harris	Gurney Slade	12	28-Dec
Cliff Richard	I love you	2	28-Dec
Ventures	Perfidia	15	28-Dec
Adam Faith	Lonely pup (in a Christmas shop)	4	28-Dec
Johnny Tillotson	Poetry in motion	5	28-Dec

The events ....

- The Queen gave birth to her third child and second son Andrew Albert Christian Edward[1]
- The Princess Margaret married photographer Antony Armstrong-Jones at Westminster Abbey in the first televised Royal marriage[2]
- Black plastic bin bags were first introduced for waste collection in Hitchin, Herts[3]
- Horncastle in Lincolnshire entered the UK Weather Records with the highest 180-min total rainfall at 178mm[6]
- The Queen launched Britain's first nuclear submarine, HMS *Dreadnought*, at Barrow-in-Furness[4]
- Michael Woodruff performed the first successful kidney transplantation in the UK, at the Edinburgh Royal Infirmary[6]
- The last man was called up for National Service as conscription ended[4,5]

HRH Princess Margaret
© Koch, Eric (1965) / Wikimedia Commons / CC BY-SA 3.0 Netherlands

HMS Dreadnought
Credit: US Navy All Hands Magazine (1960) / Wikimedia Commons / Public Domain

In the world of sport ......

- Great Britain and Northern Ireland competed at the Winter Olympics in the USA but did not win any medals[6]
- Manchester City FC signed Denis Law from Huddersfield Town for a National record fee of £55,000[7]
- The Grand National horse race was televised for the first time[8]
- Burnley FC won the Football League First Division title with a 2-1 win over Manchester City at Maine Road[9]
- Wolverhampton Wanderers won the FA Cup for the fourth time with a 3-0 win over Blackburn Rovers at Wembley Stadium[10]

- Francis Chichester arrived in New York aboard *Gypsy Moth II* having made a record solo Atlantic crossing in 40 days[6]
- Great Britain and Northern Ireland competed at the Summer Olympics in Rome and won 2 gold, 6 silver and 12 bronze medals[6]
- Vic Wilson was appointed as Yorkshire County Cricket Club's first professional captain since 1883, leading the club to the County Championship[11]

The Beatles
Credit: Billboard (1965) / Wikimedia Commons / Public Domain

In the world of entertainment........

- The Beatles performed their first concert under this name in Hamburg, Germany[12]
- Fans of traditional jazz came to blows with progressives at a jazz festival at Beaulieu, Hants in what became known as the 'Battle of Beaulieu'[13],[14]
- Ian Fleming's James Bond novel *'For Your Eyes Only'* was published[6]
- The first episode of *'Coronation Street'* was broadcast on ITV – and was still running more than 50 years later[15]
- ITV broadcasted the first live football match to be shown on television[15]
- *Lady Chatterley's Lover* sold 200,000 copies in one day following its publication having been banned since 1928[16]
- Jack Good's new TV show, *Wham!* was broadcast for the first time[17]
- Tommy Steele married former Windmill girl Ann Donoghue at St. Patrick's Church, Soho Square, London[17]
- Adam Faith became the first pop star to be interviewed on the BBC's *Face to Face*[18]
- George Formby made his final television appearance, on BBC's *The Friday Show*[17]

Adam Faith
© Phil Guest (2008) / Wikimedia Commons / CC BY-SA 2.0 Generic

George Formby with the British army in France in 1940
Credit: Puttnam L.A. (1940) / Wikimedia Commons / Public Domain

In the world of business.....

- The 18th century Naval dockyard at Sheerness on the Isle of Sheppey in Kent was closed[19]
- The daily *News Chronicle* ceased publication having been absorbed into the *Daily Mail*[20]

- The farthing, a coin first minted in England in the 13th century, ceased to be legal tender[15]
- Bill Griggs of Northampton first marketed the Dr.Martens *'AirWair'* style 1460 boots[21]

In the world of transport.....

- The Avro 748 made its first flight at Woodford[6]
- The Bluebell Railway in Sussex began regular operation as the first standard gauge steam-operated passenger heritage railway in the world[22]
- The first traffic wardens were deployed in London[15]
- The Sheffield Tramway closed leaving Blackpool as the only place in England with electric trams[23]

Dr. Martens Airwair
Credit: Vugluskr (2005)
/ Wikimedia Commons /
Public Domain

1961

Welcome to the lighter side of life in Britain in 1961

The music ……

Artist	Title	Highest position this year	W/E date
Shirley Bassey	As long as he needs me	17	04-Jan
Johnny Burnette	Dreamin'	18	04-Jan
Max Harris	Gurney Slade	11	04-Jan
Cliff Richard	I love you	1	04-Jan
Elvis Presley	It's now or never	2	04-Jan
Nina & Frederik	Little donkey	4	04-Jan
Connie Francis	My heart has a mind of its own	10	04-Jan
Frank Sinatra	Ol' Mac Donald	20	04-Jan
Johnny & The Hurricanes	Rocking goose	8	04-Jan
Anthony Newley	Strawberry fair	3	04-Jan
Lonnie Donegan	Lively	14	11-Jan
Adam Faith	Lonely pup (in a Christmas shop)	4	11-Jan
Johnny Mathis	My love for you	17	11-Jan
Drifters	Save the last dance for me	2	11-Jan
Peter Sellers & Sophia Loren	Goodness gracious me	6	18-Jan
Shadows	Man of mystery / The stranger	7	18-Jan
Johnny Tillotson	Poetry in motion	1	18-Jan
Roy Orbison	Blue angel	14	25-Jan
Everly Brothers	Like strangers	11	25-Jan
Marty Wilde	Little girl	16	25-Jan
Ventures	Perfidia	4	25-Jan
Matt Monro	Portrait of my love	3	25-Jan
Andy Stewart	A Scottish soldier (green hills of Tyrol)	19	01-Feb

Artist	Song	#	Date
Bobby Rydell	Sway	12	01-Feb
Elvis Presley	Are you lonesome tonight?	1	01-Feb
Emile Ford & The Checkmates	Counting teardrops	4	01-Feb
Maurice Williams & The Zodiacs	Stay	14	01-Feb
Connie Francis	Many tears ago	12	08-Feb
Duane Eddy	Pepe	2	08-Feb
Billy Fury	A thousand stars	14	15-Feb
Russ Conway	Pepe	19	15-Feb
Anne Shelton	Sailor	10	15-Feb
Mr Acker Bilk & His Paramount Jazz Band	Buona Sera	7	22-Feb
Shadows	F.B.I.	6	22-Feb
Piltdown Men	Piltdown rides again	14	22-Feb
Marty Wilde	Rubber ball	9	22-Feb
Bobby Vee	Rubber ball	4	22-Feb
Johnny Burnette	You're sixteen	3	22-Feb
Gary U.S.Bonds	New Orleans	16	01-Mar
Petula Clark	Sailor	1	01-Mar
Adam Faith	Who am I / This is it	5	01-Mar
Neil Sedaka	Calender girl	8	08-Mar
Benny Hill	Gather in the mushrooms	12	08-Mar
Jess Conrad	Mystery girl	18	08-Mar
Everly Brothers	Walk right back / Ebony eyes	1	08-Mar
Allisons	Are you sure?	2	15-Mar
Johnny & The Hurricanes	Ja-da	14	15-Mar
Brenda Lee	Let's jump the broomstick	12	15-Mar
Shirelles	Will you still love me tomorrow?	4	15-Mar
Cliff Richard	Theme for a dream	3	22-Mar
String-a-longs	Wheels	8	22-Mar
Mike Preston	Marry me	14	29-Mar
Matt Monro	My kind of girl	5	29-Mar
Ramrods	Riders in the sky	8	29-Mar
Elvis Presley	Wooden heart	1	29-Mar

Artist	Title		Date
Kenny Ball & His Jazzmen	Samantha	13	05-Apr
King Brothers	76 Trombones	19	12-Apr
Buzz Clifford	Baby sittin' boogie	17	12-Apr
Piltdown Men	Goodnight Mrs.Flintstone	18	12-Apr
Anthony Newley	And the heaven's cried	6	19-Apr
Ferrante & Teicher	Theme from 'Exodus'	6	26-Apr
Bobby Darin	Lazy river	2	03-May
Connie Francis	Where the boys are / Baby Roo	5	03-May
Johnny Dankworth	African waltz	9	10-May
Marcels	Blue moon	1	10-May
Cliff Richard	Gee whizz it's you	4	10-May
Brook Brothers	War paint	5	10-May
Craig Douglas	A hundred pounds of clay	9	17-May
Helen Shapiro	Don't treat me like a child	3	17-May
Johnny Burnette	Little boy sad	12	17-May
Bobby Vee	More than I can say / Staying in	4	17-May
Duane Eddy	Theme from Dixie	7	17-May
Adam Faith	Easy going me	12	24-May
Floyd Cramer	On the rebound	1	24-May
Temperance Seven	You're driving me crazy	1	31-May
Elvis Presley	Surrender	1	07-Jun
Shadows	The frightened city	3	07-Jun
Jerry Lee Lewis	What'd I say	10	07-Jun
Lonnie Donegan	Have a drink on me	8	21-Jun
Shirley Bassey	You'll never know	6	21-Jun
Neil Sedaka	Little devil	9	28-Jun
Clarence 'Frogman' Henry	(I don't know why I love you) But I do	3	28-Jun
Linda Scott	I've told every little star	7	28-Jun
Temperance Seven	Pasadena	4	05-Jul
Anthony Newley	Pop goes the weasel / Bee bom	12	05-Jul
Del Shannon	Runaway	1	05-Jul

Artist	Title	#	Date
Roy Orbison	Runnin' scared	9	05-Jul
Ricky Nelson	Hello Mary Lou / Travellin' Man	2	12-Jul
Duane Eddy	Ring of fire	17	12-Jul
Cliff Richard	A girl like you	3	26-Jul
Connie Francis	Breakin' a brand new broken heart	12	26-Jul
Everly Brothers	Temptation	1	26-Jul
Eddie Cochran	Weekend	15	26-Jul
Pat Boone	Moody river	18	02-Aug
Craig Douglas	Time	9	02-Aug
Adam Faith	Don't you know it?	12	09-Aug
Billy Fury	Halfway to Paradise	3	09-Aug
Eden Kane	Well I ask you	1	09-Aug
Buddy Holly	Baby I don't care / Valley of tears	12	16-Aug
Clarence 'Frogman' Henry	You always hurt the one you love	6	16-Aug
Helen Shapiro	You don't know	1	16-Aug
Petula Clark	Romeo	3	30-Aug
John Leyton	Johnny remember me	1	06-Sep
Karl Denver	Marcheta	8	06-Sep
Gary U.S.Bonds	Quarter to three	7	06-Sep
Mr Acker Bilk & His Paramount Jazz Band	That's my home	7	13-Sep
Elvis Presley	Wild in the country / I feel so bad	4	20-Sep
Bobby Vee	How many tears	10	20-Sep
Brook Brothers	Ain't gonna wash for a week	13	20-Sep
Sam Cooke	Cupid	7	27-Sep
Lonnie Donegan	Michael, row the boat / Lumbered	6	27-Sep
Shirley Bassey	Reach for the stars / Climb ev'ry mountain	1	27-Sep
Eden Kane	Get lost	10	11-Oct
Billy Fury	Jealousy	2	11-Oct
Shadows	Kon-Tiki	1	11-Oct
Don Gibson	Sea of heartbreak	14	11-Oct

Artist	Title		Date
Highwaymen	Michael	1	18-Oct
Connie Francis	Together	6	18-Oct
Frank Sinatra	Granada	15	25-Oct
Everly Brothers	Muskrat / Don't blame me	20	25-Oct
Helen Shapiro	Walking back to happiness	1	25-Oct
Cleo Laine	You'll answer to me	5	25-Oct
Del Shannon	Hats off to Larry	6	01-Nov
Laurie Johnson Orchestra	Sucu sucu	9	01-Nov
John Leyton	Wild wind	2	01-Nov
Tony Orlando	Bless you	5	08-Nov
Karl Denver	Mexicali Rose	8	08-Nov
Cliff Richard	When the girl in your arms is the girl in your heart	3	08-Nov
Bobby Darin	You must have been a beautiful baby	10	08-Nov
Ray Charles	Hit the road Jack	6	15-Nov
Elvis Presley	Little sister / (Marie's the name of) His latest flame	1	15-Nov
Charlie Drake	My boomerang won't come back	14	22-Nov
Dave Brubeck Quartet	Take five	6	22-Nov
Jimmy Dean	Big bad John	2	29-Nov
Hayley Mills	Let's get together	17	29-Nov
Adam Faith	The time has come	4	29-Nov
Dion	Runaround Sue	11	06-Dec
Shadows	The savage	10	06-Dec
Jimmy Crawford	I love how you love me	18	13-Dec
Shirley Bassey	I'll get by (as long as I have you)	10	13-Dec
Frankie Vaughan	Tower of strength	1	13-Dec
Jim Reeves	You're the only good thing (that happened to me)	17	20-Dec
G-Clefs	I understand (just how you feel)	19	20-Dec

Springfields	Bambino	16	20-Dec
Danny Williams	Moon river	2	20-Dec
Bobby Vee	Take good care of my baby	3	20-Dec
Pat Boone	Johnny will	4	27-Dec
Sandy Nelson	Let there be drums	15	27-Dec
Kenny Ball & His Jazzmen	Midnight in Moscow	5	27-Dec
Petula Clark	My friend the sea	7	27-Dec
Del Shannon	So long baby	11	27-Dec
Mr Acker Bilk & His Paramount Jazz Band	Stranger on the shore	6	27-Dec
Russ Conway	Toy balloons	14	27-Dec

The events ……..

- Black & white £5 notes ceased to be legal tender in the UK[33]
- Prince Edward, Duke of Kent, married Katharine Worsley at York Minster[27]

In the world of sport ……

- Tottenham Hotspur won the Football League Division One title with a 2-1 win over Sheffield Wednesday[24]
- Tottenham Hotspur became the first English football team this century to win the double of the league title and the FA cup, with a 2-0 win over Leicester City in the FA cup final at Wembley Stadium[25]
- Angela Mortimer beat Christine Truman in an all-British women's final at the Wimbledon Tennis Championships[26]

In the world of entertainment……..

- The TV series *'The Avengers'* was first screened on ITV[27]
- The Shakespeare Memorial Theatre, Stratford-upon-Avon, became the Royal Shakespeare Theatre and its company the Royal Shakespeare Company[28]
- The Beatles performed at Liverpool's Cavern Club for the first time[27]
- Ian Fleming's James Bond novel *'Thunderball'* was published[27]
- Welsh-born Rosemarie Frankland became the first British winner of the Miss World beauty pageant in London[27]
- Muriel Spark's short novel *The Prime of Miss Jean Brodie* was published[27]
- The first edition of the magazine *'Private Eye'* was published[33]
- *'Songs of Praise'* was first broadcast on the BBC[27]
- The musical film *'The Young Ones'* was released starring Cliff Richard[29]

In the world of business.....

- The first Mothercare shop opened in Kingston-upon-Thames[30]
- Barclay's opened their 'No.1 Computer Centre' in Drummond Street, London with an EMI mainframe computer[31],[32]
- *'The Sunday Telegraph'* was first published[33]
- Betting shops were legalized under the terms of the Betting and Gaming Act 1960[34]
- The United Kingdom became a member of the OECD[35]
- Britain applied for membership in the EEC[27]
- In a referendum on the Sunday opening of public houses in Wales, the counties of Anglesey, Cardiganshire, Caernarfonshire, Carmarthenshire, Denbighshire, Merionethshire, Montgomeryshire and Pembrokeshire all voted to stay "dry"[27]

In the world of transport.....

- The government unveiled new 'panda' crossings with push button controls for pedestrians with deployment scheduled the following year[36]
- The Jaguar E-Type, a sports car capable of 150 mph, was launched as a two-seater roadster or 2+2 coupe[37]

Jaguar e-Type
© Dan Smith (2005) / Wikimedia Commons / CC BY-SA 2.5 Generic

1962

Welcome to the lighter side of life in Britain in 1962

The music ……

Artist	Title	Highest position this year	W/E date
Jimmy Dean	Big bad John	12	03-Jan
Dorothy Provine	Don't bring Lulu	17	03-Jan
Shirley Bassey	I'll get by	19	03-Jan
Elvis Presley	Little sister / (Marie's the name of) His latest flame	13	03-Jan
Kenny Ball & His Jazzmen	Midnight in Moscow	2	03-Jan
Danny Williams	Moon river	1	03-Jan
Mrs. Mills	Mrs. Mills medley	18	03-Jan
Petula Clark	My friend the sea	9	03-Jan
Bobby Vee	Take good care of my baby	8	03-Jan
Russ Conway	Toy balloons	7	03-Jan
G-Clefs	I understand (just how you feel)	17	10-Jan
Pat Boone	Johnny will	4	10-Jan
Sandy Nelson	Let there be drums	3	10-Jan
Shadows	The savage	20	10-Jan
Frankie Vaughan	Tower of strength	2	10-Jan
Helen Shapiro	Walking back to happiness	13	10-Jan
Billy Fury	I'd never find another you	5	17-Jan
Del Shannon	So long baby	10	17-Jan
Mr. Acker Bilk & His Paramount Jazz Band	Stranger on the shore	2	17-Jan
Jim Reeves	You're the only good thing (that happened to me)	18	17-Jan
Cliff Richard	The young ones	1	17-Jan

Artist	Title		Date
Tokens	The lion sleeps tonight (Wimoweh)	11	17-Jan
John Leyton	Son, this is she	15	24-Jan
John D.Loudermilk	The language of love	13	24-Jan
Chubby Checker	The twist	14	24-Jan
Neil Sedaka	Happy birthday, sweet sixteen	3	31-Jan
Bobby Darin	Multiplication	5	31-Jan
Chubby Checker	Let's twist again	2	07-Feb
Eden Kane	Forget me not	3	14-Feb
Adam Faith	Lonesome	12	14-Feb
Lonnie Donegan	The Comancheros	14	14-Feb
Leroy Van Dyke	Walk on by	5	14-Feb
Bobby Vee	Run to him	6	21-Feb
Burl Ives	A little bitty tear	9	28-Feb
Danny Williams	Jeannie	14	28-Feb
Elvis Presley	Rock-a-hula baby / Can't help falling in love	1	28-Feb
Everly Brothers	I'll do my crying in the rain	6	07-Mar
Miki & Griff	A little bitty tear	16	14-Mar
Karl Denver	Wimoweh	4	14-Mar
Kenny Ball & His Jazzmen	March of the Siamese children	4	28-Mar
Helen Shapiro	Tell me what he said	2	28-Mar
Dion & The Belmonts	The wanderer	10	28-Mar
Shadows	Wonderful land	1	28-Mar
Bernard Cribbins	Hole in the ground	9	04-Apr
Matt Monro	Softly as I leave you	10	04-Apr
Paul Anka	Love me warm and tender	19	11-Apr
Roy Orbison	Dream baby	2	18-Apr
Johnny Spence	Theme from 'Dr.Kildare'	15	18-Apr
Sam Cooke	Twistin' the night away	6	18-Apr
Karl Denver	Never goodbye	9	25-Apr
Joe Loss & His Orchestra	Theme from 'Maigret'	20	25-Apr
Johnny Keating Orchestra	Theme from 'Z-Cars'	8	25-Apr

Bruce Chanel	Hey! Baby	2	02-May
Craig Douglas	When my little girl is smiling	9	02-May
Del Shannon	Hey! Little girl	2	09-May
Ricky Nelson	Young world	19	09-May
Brenda Lee	Speak to me pretty	3	16-May
Lonnie Donegan	The party's over	9	16-May
Danny Williams	Wonderful world of the young	8	16-May
B.Bumble & The Stingers	Nut rocker	1	23-May
Jimmy Justice	When my little girl is smiling	9	23-May
Adam Faith	As you like it	5	30-May
Elvis Presley	Good luck charm	1	30-May
Ketty Lester	Love letters	4	30-May
Cliff Richard	Do you want to dance / I'm looking out the window	2	06-Jun
Billy Fury	Last night was made for love	4	06-Jun
Everly Brothers	How can I meet her	12	20-Jun
Eden Kane	I don't know why	7	20-Jun
Marty Wilde	Jezebel	19	20-Jun
John Leyton	Lonely city	14	20-Jun
Vernons Girls	Lover please / You know what I mean	16	20-Jun
Duane Eddy	Deep in the heart of Texas	19	27-Jun
Brian Hyland	Ginny come lately	5	27-Jun
Richard Chamberlain	Theme from 'Dr.Kildare' (Three stars will shine tonight)	12	27-Jun
Dave Brubeck	Unsquare dance	14	27-Jun
Karl Denver	A little love, a little kiss	19	04-Jul
Joe Brown	A picture of you	2	04-Jul
Mike Sarne & Wendy Richard	Come outside	1	04-Jul
Jimmy Justice	Ain't that funny	8	11-Jul
Bobby Vee	Sharing you	10	11-Jul

Artist	Song	Pos	Date
Kenny Ball & His Jazzmen	The green leaves of summer	7	11-Jul
Ray Charles	I can't stop loving you	1	18-Jul
Freddy Cannon	Palisades Park	20	18-Jul
Eydie Gorme	Yes my darling daughter	10	18-Jul
Jimmy Rodgers	English country garden	5	25-Jul
Craig Douglas	Our favourite melodies	9	25-Jul
Brenda Lee	Here comes that feeling	5	01-Aug
Frank Ifield	I remember you	1	01-Aug
Petula Clark	Ya Ya twist	14	01-Aug
Shane Fenton & The Fentones	Cindy's birthday	19	08-Aug
Buddy Holly & The Crickets	Don't ever change	5	08-Aug
Nat 'King' Cole & The George Shearing Quartet	Let there be love	11	08-Aug
Helen Shapiro	Little Miss Lonely	8	08-Aug
Bernard Cribbins	Right, said Fred	10	08-Aug
Pat Boone	Speedy Gonzales	2	15-Aug
Shadows	Guitar tango	4	22-Aug
Billy Fury	Once upon a dream	7	22-Aug
Bobby Vinton	Roses are red (my love)	15	29-Aug
Chubby Checker	Dancin' party	19	05-Sep
Louise Cordet	I'm just a baby	13	05-Sep
Kenny Ball & His Jazzmen	So do I	14	05-Sep
Connie Francis	V.A.C.A.T.I.O.N.	10	05-Sep
Neil Sedaka	Breaking up is hard to do	7	12-Sep
Brian Hyland	Sealed with a kiss	3	12-Sep
Lonnie Donegan	Pick a bale of cotton	11	12-Sep
Bobby Darin	Things	2	12-Sep
Duane Eddy	Ballad of Paladin	10	19-Sep
Ronnie Carroll	Roses are red (my love)	3	19-Sep

Elvis Presley	She's not you	1	19-Sep
Jimmy Justice	Spanish Harlem	20	19-Sep
Jet Harris	Theme from 'The Man With The Golden Arm'	12	19-Sep
Mike Sarne	Will I what?	18	19-Sep
Adam Faith	Don't that beat all	8	03-Oct
Cliff Richard	It'll be me	2	03-Oct
Tornados	Telstar	1	10-Oct
Ray Charles	You don't know me	9	10-Oct
Brenda Lee	It started all over again	15	17-Oct
Buddy Holly	Reminiscing	17	17-Oct
Tommy Roe	Sheila	3	17-Oct
Little Eva	The loco-motion	2	17-Oct
Carole King	It might as well rain until September	3	24-Oct
Mr. Acker Bilk & His Paramount Jazz Band	Lonely	14	24-Oct
Shirley Bassey	What now my love?	5	24-Oct
Nat 'King' Cole	Ramblin' Rose	5	31-Oct
Chris Montez	Let's dance	2	07-Nov
Mark Wynter	Venus in blue jeans	4	07-Nov
Billy Fury	Because of love	18	14-Nov
Frank Ifield	Lovesick blues	1	14-Nov
Joe Loss & His Orchestra	Must be Madison	20	21-Nov
Four Seasons	Sherry	8	28-Nov
Susan Maughan	Bobby's girl	3	05-Dec
Duane Eddy	Dance with the guitar man	6	05-Dec
Marty Robbins	Devil woman	5	05-Dec
Craig Douglas	Oh, lonesome me	15	05-Dec
Everly Brothers	No one can make my sunshine smile	11	05-Dec
Del Shannon	The Swiss maid	2	05-Dec
John Barry Orchestra	Theme from 'James Bond'	13	12-Dec
Bobby Vee	A forever kind of love	17	19-Dec
Stan Getz & Charlie Byrd	Desafinado	13	19-Dec

Beatles	Love me do	19	19-Dec
Elvis Presley	Return to sender	1	19-Dec
Rolf Harris	Sun arise	3	19-Dec
Pat Boone	The main attraction	12	19-Dec
Shadows	Dance on!	11	26-Dec
Joe Brown	It only took a minute	13	26-Dec
Maureen Evans	Like I do	20	26-Dec
Richard Chamberlain	Love me tender	15	26-Dec
Brenda Lee	Rockin' around the Christmas tree	7	26-Dec
Cliff Richard	The next time / Bachelor boy	2	26-Dec

The events ……..

- The new Coventry Cathedral was consecrated[47]
- Britain's first legal casino opened in Brighton, Sussex[38]
- John Charnley completed the world's first successful whole hip replacement operation at Wrightington Hospital, Wigan[39]
- The last permanent inhabitants left the island of Stroma, Scotland[41]
- The "Big Freeze" gripped Britain with no frost-free nights from December until March 1963[41]
- Elizabeth Lane was appointed as the first female County Court judge[41]

Coventry Cathedral
© Cmglee (2011) / Wikimedia Commons / CC BY-SA 3.0 Unported

In the world of sport ……

- Accrington Stanley resigned from the Football League due to huge debts[40]
- Ipswich Town won the Football League First Division title[41]
- Tottenham Hotspur retained the FA Cup with a 3-1 win over Burnley at Wembley Stadium[41]
- Oxford United F.C., champions of the Southern League, were elected to the Football League in place of bankrupt Accrington Stanley[41]
- Mountaineers Chris Bonington and Ian Clough became the first Britons to climb the north face of the Eiger[47]

In the world of entertainment……..

- The BBC broadcast the first episode of 'Z-Cars'[41]

- The Beatles auditioned for Decca Records in West Hampstead, London where Dick Rowe turned them down in favour of Brian Poole & The Tremeloes[42]
- Brian Epstein signed a contract to manage the Beatles[42]
- The Beatles played their first session at Abbey Road Studios[43]
- The first episode of *'Steptoe & Son'* was broadcast by the BBC[41]
- Live television was broadcast for the first time from the USA to Britain via the Telstar satellite and the Goonhilly Satellite Earth Station[44]
- The Rolling Stones made their debut at London's Marquee Club, opening for Long John Baldry[41]
- The Beatles played their first live engagement with the line-up of John, Paul, George & Ringo at Hulme Hall, Port Sunlight[43]
- John Lennon secretly married Cynthia Powell at Mount Pleasant, Liverpool[41]
- Channel Television, the ITV franchise for the Channel Islands, went on the air[41]
- Wales West and North Television went on the air to the North and West Wales region, extending ITV to the whole of the UK[41]
- *'University Challenge'* was first broadcast[47]
- *'Dr.No'*, the first James Bond film was released with Sean Connery in the lead role[45]
- The Beatles made their first televised appearance on *'People and Places'*[47]
- Anthony Burgess's novel *'A Clockwork Orange'* was first published[41]
- Len Deighton's novel *The IPCRESS File* was first published[41]
- Ian Fleming's James Bond novel *'The Spy Who Loved Me'* was published[41]
- David Lean's film *'Lawrence of Arabia'* was released[41]
- The *Record Mirror* stopped compiling its own chart and began publishing the chart from *Record Retailer* instead[46]

In the world of business…..

- *The Sunday Times* became the first paper to print a colour supplement[47]
- The company Golden Wonder introduced the first flavoured crisps (cheese and onion) to the UK market[48]
- Safeway opened its first supermarket in Bedford[49]

In the world of transport…..

- The last trolleybuses ran in London[50]
- The world's first regular passenger hovercraft service was introduced between Rhyl in North Wales and Wallasey[47]
- Glasgow Corporation Tramways ran its last cars in normal service, leaving the Blackpool tramway as the last remaining in Britain[41]
- Ford launched the Cortina in competition to the Vauxhall Victor, Hillman Minx and Morris Oxford Farina[51]

- An agreement was signed between Britain and France to develop the *Concorde* supersonic airliner[47]
- Britain's motorway network expanded with the completion of the first phases of the M5 and M6[52]

London trolleybus
© *Bahnfrend (2014) / Wikimedia Commons /*
CC BY-SA 4.0 International

Ford Cortina Mk 1
© *Duncan Harris (2009) / Wikimedia*
Commons /

1963

Welcome to the lighter side of life in Britain in 1963

The music ……

Artist	Title	Highest position this year	W/E date
Duane Eddy & The Rebelettes	Dance with the guitar man	4	02-Jan
Stan Getz & Charlie Byrd	Desafinado	11	02-Jan
Marty Robbins	Devil woman	14	02-Jan
Chris Montez	Let's dance	10	02-Jan
Beatles	Love me do	17	02-Jan
Frank Sinatra & Sammy Davis Jr.	Me and my shadow	20	02-Jan
Elvis Presley	Return to sender	1	02-Jan
Brenda Lee	Rockin' around the Christmas tree	6	02-Jan
Tornados	Telstar	8	02-Jan
Pat Boone	The main attraction	16	02-Jan
Hank Locklin	We're gonna go fishin'	18	02-Jan
Ray Charles	Your cheating heart	13	02-Jan
Bobby Vee	A forever kind of love	13	09-Jan
Susan Maughan	Bobby's girl	6	09-Jan
Frank Ifield	Lovesick blues	3	09-Jan
Rolf Harris	Sun arise	4	09-Jan
Cliff Richard	The next time / Bachelor boy	1	09-Jan
Del Shannon	The Swiss maid	11	09-Jan
Crystals	He's a rebel	19	16-Jan
Joe Brown	It only took a minute	6	16-Jan
Mark Wynter	Go away little girl	6	23-Jan
Mel Torme	Coming home baby	13	30-Jan
Shadows	Dance on!	1	30-Jan

Tornados	Globetrotter	5	30-Jan
Maureen Evans	Like I do	3	30-Jan
Kenny Lynch	Up on the roof	10	30-Jan
Four Seasons	Big girls don't cry	13	06-Feb
Jet Harris & Tony Meehan	Diamonds	1	06-Feb
Mike Berry & The Outlaws	Don't you think it's time?	6	06-Feb
Chris Montez	Some kinda fun	10	06-Feb
Mr. Acker Bilk & His Paramount Jazz Band	A taste of honey	16	13-Feb
Del Shannon	Little town flirt	4	20-Feb
Crickets	My little girl	17	20-Feb
Kenny Ball & His Jazzmen	Sukiyaki	10	20-Feb
Brenda Lee	All alone am I	7	27-Feb
Beatles	Please please me	2	27-Feb
Frank Ifield	The wayward wind	1	27-Feb
Spotnicks	Hava Nagila	13	06-Mar
Frankie Vaughan	Loop-de-loop	5	06-Mar
Bobby Vee	The night has a thousand eyes	3	06-Mar
Richard Chamberlain	Hi-lili hi-lo	20	13-Mar
Rooftop Singers	Walk right in	10	13-Mar
Paul & Paula	Hey Paula	8	20-Mar
Elvis Presley	One broken heart for sale	12	20-Mar
Cliff Richard	Summer holiday	1	20-Mar
Billie Davis	Tell him	10	20-Mar
Joe Brown	That's what love will do	3	20-Mar
Bachelors	Charmaine	6	03-Apr
Shadows	Foot tapper	1	03-Apr
Springfields	Island of dreams	5	03-Apr
Billy Fury	Like I've never been gone	3	03-Apr
Ronnie Carroll	Say wonderful things	6	10-Apr
Ned Miller	From a Jack to a King	2	17-Apr
Gerry & The Pacemakers	How do you do it?	1	17-Apr
Little Eva	Let's turkey trot	13	17-Apr
Cascades	Rhythm of the rain	5	17-Apr

Artist	Title		Date
Buddy Holly	Brown-eyed handsome man	3	24-Apr
Tornados	Robot	17	24-Apr
Tommy Roe	The folk singer	4	24-Apr
Springfields	Say I won't be there	5	01-May
Skeeter Davis	The end of the world	18	01-May
Four Seasons	Walk like a man	12	01-May
Beatles	From me to you	1	08-May
Frank Ifield	Nobody's darlin' but mine	4	08-May
Chiffons	He's so fine	16	15-May
Roy Orbison	In dreams	6	15-May
Brenda Lee	Losing you	10	15-May
Andy Williams	Can't get used to losing you	2	22-May
Del Shannon	Two kinds of teardrops	5	22-May
Cliff Richard	Lucky lips	4	29-May
Jet Harris & Tony Meehan	Scarlett O'Hara	2	29-May
Paul & Paula	Young lovers	9	29-May
Billy J.Kramer & The Dakotas	Do you want to know a secret?	2	05-Jun
Benny Hill	Harvest of love	20	05-Jun
Chantays	Pipeline	16	12-Jun
Ray Charles	Take these chains from my heart	5	12-Jun
Billy Fury	When will you say I love you	3	12-Jun
Gerry & The Pacemakers	I like it	1	26-Jun
Freddie & The Dreamers	If you gotta make a fool of somebody	3	26-Jun
Shadows	Atlantis	2	03-Jul
Roy Orbison	Falling	9	03-Jul
Tornados	The Ice Cream man	18	03-Jul
Wink Martindale	Deck of cards	5	10-Jul
Bobby Rydell	Forget him	13	10-Jul
Buddy Holly	Bo Diddley	4	17-Jul
Lesley Gore	It's my party	9	17-Jul
Jim Reeves	Welcome to my world	6	17-Jul

Artist	Title	Pos	Date
Frank Ifield	Confessin' (that I love you)	1	24-Jul
Crystals	Da doo ron ron	5	24-Jul
Elvis Presley	(You're the) Devil in disguise	1	07-Aug
Brenda Lee	I wonder	14	07-Aug
Brian Poole & The Tremeloes	Twist and shout	4	07-Aug
Kyu Sakamoto	Sukiyaki	6	14-Aug
Searchers	Sweets for my sweet	1	14-Aug
Kenny Lynch	You can never stop me loving you	10	14-Aug
Billy J.Kramer & The Dakotas	Bad to me	1	28-Aug
Billy Fury	In summer	5	28-Aug
Freddie & The Dreamers	I'm tellin' you now	2	04-Sep
Ken Thorne	Theme from 'The Legion's Last Patrol'	4	04-Sep
Surfaris	Wipe out	5	04-Sep
Dakotas	The cruel sea	18	11-Sep
Kathy Kirby	Dance on	11	18-Sep
Johnny Kidd & The Pirates	I'll never get over you	4	18-Sep
Cliff Richard	It's all in the game	2	18-Sep
Beatles	She loves you	1	18-Sep
Karl Denver	Still	13	18-Sep
Caravelles	You don't have to be a baby to cry	6	18-Sep
Bachelors	Whispering	18	25-Sep
Jet Harris & Tony Meehan	Applejack	4	02-Oct
Steve Lawrence & Eydie Gorme	I want to stay here	3	02-Oct
Heinz	Just like Eddie	5	02-Oct
Buddy Holly	Wishing	10	02-Oct
Brian Poole & The Tremeloes	Do you love me?	1	16-Oct
Trini Lopez	If I had a hammer	4	16-Oct
Hollies	Searchin'	12	16-Oct
Shadows	Shindig	6	16-Oct
Billy Fury	Somebody else's girl	18	16-Oct

Crystals	Then he kissed me	2	16-Oct
Tommy Roe	Everybody	9	23-Oct
Adam Faith	The first time	5	23-Oct
Fourmost	Hello little girl	9	30-Oct
Allan Sherman	Hello Muddah! Hello Fadduh!	14	30-Oct
Shirley Bassey	I (who have nothing)	6	30-Oct
Elvis Presley	Bossa Nova baby	13	06-Nov
Gerry & The Pacemakers	You'll never walk alone	1	06-Nov
Roy Orbison	Blue Bayou / Mean woman blues	3	13-Nov
Ricky Nelson	Fools rush in	12	13-Nov
Dave Berry & The Cruisers	Memphis Tennessee	19	13-Nov
Jimmy Young	Miss you	15	13-Nov
Chuck Berry	Let it rock / Memphis Tennessee	6	20-Nov
Searchers	Sugar and spice	2	20-Nov
Ronettes	Be my baby	4	27-Nov
Peter, Paul & Mary	Blowing in the wind	13	04-Dec
Matt Monro	From Russia with love	20	04-Dec
Billy J.Kramer & The Dakotas	I'll keep you satisfied	4	04-Dec
Nino Tempo & April Stevens	Deep purple	17	11-Dec
Johnny Kidd & The Pirates	Hungry for love	20	11-Dec
Freddie & The Dreamers	You were made for me	3	11-Dec
Mark Wynter	It's almost tomorrow	12	11-Dec
Cliff Richard	Don't talk to him	2	11-Dec
Beatles	I want to hold your hand	1	18-Dec
Los Indios Tagajaras	Maria Elena	5	18-Dec
Kathy Kirby	Secret love	4	18-Dec
Hollies	Stay	17	18-Dec
Singing Nun	Dominique	8	25-Dec
Shadows	Geronimo	11	25-Dec
Dave Clark Five	Glad all over	4	25-Dec
Rolling Stones	I wanna be your man	13	25-Dec

Dusty Springfield	I only want to be with you	6	25-Dec
Harry Secombe	If I ruled the world	18	25-Dec
Bern Elliott & The Fenmen	Money	14	25-Dec
Chris Sandford	Not too little - not too much	17	25-Dec
Big Dee Irwin	Swinging on a star	15	25-Dec
Gene Pitney	Twenty four hours from Tulsa	9	25-Dec

The events ....

- Britain had the worst winter since 1946/47[53]
- Princess Alexandra of Kent married the Hon Angus Ogilvy at Westminster Abbey[53]
- The Great Train Robbery took place in Buckinghamshire[54]

In the world of sport ......

- Everton won the Football League First Division title[55]
- Tottenham Hotspur became the first British football team to win a European trophy with a 5-1 win over Atletico Madrid in Rotterdam to take the European Cup Winners' Cup[53]
- Manchester United beat Leicester City 3-1 in the FA Cup final at Wembley Stadium[56]

In the world of entertainment.......

- Granada TV first broadcast *'World in Action'*[53]
- The musical film *'Summer Holiday'* starring Cliff Richard received its London premiere[53]
- The first episode of *'Doctor Who'* was broadcast by the BBC[63]
- Ian Fleming's James Bond novel *'On Her Majesty's Secret Service'* was published[53]
- John le Carre's novel *'The Spy Who Came in From the Cold'* was published[53]
- Alastair MacLean's thriller *'Ice Station Zebra'* was published[53]
- Having seen the band in concert in London the previous day, Andrew Loog Oldham signed a contract with The Rolling Stones to become their manager[57]
- The Beatles performed at the Cavern Club for the last time[57]

Cliff Richard
© *Dutch National Archives (1962) / Wikimedia Commons / CC BY-SA 3.0 Netherlands*

- *The Daily Mirror* used the term "Beatlemania" for the first time in an article about the groups concert in Cheltenham, England[57]
- The musical film *'What a Crazy World'* starring Joe Brown was released[57]
- The Springfields played their last concert at the London Palladium and Dusty Springfield released her first solo single[57]

'Beatlemania' at Schipol Airport in Denmark
© *Dutch National Archive (1964) / Wikimedia Commons / CC BY-SA 3.0 Nertherlands*

In the world of business.....

- Charles de Gaulle, President of France, vetoed the UK's entry into the European Economic Community[53]
- The Sindy fashion doll was first marketed by Pedigree[58,59,60]
- S. Hille & Co marketed the Polypropylene stacking chair designed by Robin Day[61]

In the world of education.....

- The University of East Anglia opened in Norwich[53]

Dusty Springfield
Credit: Billboard (1966) / Wikimedia Commons / Public Domain

In the world of transport.....

- The Vauxhall Viva was launched[62]
- The Dartford Tunnel opened in Essex[63]
- The new Rover P6 from BMC was the first winner of the European Car of the Year award[53]

Rover P6
© *Lars-Goran Lindgren Sweden (2007) / Wikimedia Commons / CC BY-SA 3.0 Unported*

Vauxhall HA Viva
© *Charles01 (2015) / Wikimedia Commons / CC BY-SA 4.0 International*

- The first sections of the M4 in Berkshire, the M6 between Warrington and Preston, and the M2 in Kent were opened[64]

1964

Welcome to the lighter side of life in Britain in 1964

The music ……

Artist	Title	Highest position this year	W/E date
Dora Bryan	All I want for Christmas is a Beatle	20	01-Jan
Singing Nun	Dominique	7	01-Jan
Cliff Richard	Don't talk to him	8	01-Jan
Shadows	Geronimo	11	01-Jan
Beatles	I want to hold your hand	1	01-Jan
Billy J. Kramer & The Dakotas	I'll keep you satisfied	13	01-Jan
Bern Elliott & The Fenmen	Money	19	01-Jan
Chris Sandford	Not too little - not too much	18	01-Jan
Kathy Kirby	Secret love	4	01-Jan
Beatles	She loves you	2	01-Jan
Freddie & The Dreamers	You were made for me	3	01-Jan
Gerry & The Pacemakers	You'll never walk alone	12	01-Jan
Elvis Presley	Kiss me quick	14	08-Jan
Los Indios Tagajaras	Maria Elena	8	08-Jan
Gene Pitney	Twenty four hours from Tulsa	5	08-Jan
Dusty Springfield	I only want to be with you	4	15-Jan
Rolling Stones	I wanna be your man	12	15-Jan
Dave Clark Five	Glad all over	1	22-Jan
Hollies	Stay	8	22-Jan
Big Dee Irwin	Swinging on a star	7	22-Jan
Swinging Blue Jeans	Hippy hippy shake	2	29-Jan
Adam Faith	We are in love	11	29-Jan

Artist	Title	Weeks	Date
Billy Fury	Do you really love me too?	13	05-Feb
Searchers	Needles and pins	1	05-Feb
Brenda Lee	As usual	5	12-Feb
Fourmost	I'm in love	17	12-Feb
Gerry & The Pacemakers	I'm the one	2	12-Feb
Nino Tempo & April Stevens	Whispering	20	12-Feb
Manfred Mann	5-4-3-2-1	5	19-Feb
Frank Ifield	Don't blame me	8	19-Feb
Bachelors	Diane	1	26-Feb
Ricky Nelson	For you	14	26-Feb
Cliff Richard	I'm the lonely one	8	26-Feb
Cilla Black	Anyone who had a heart	1	04-Mar
Ronettes	Baby, I love you	11	04-Mar
Merseybeats	I think of you	5	04-Mar
Dave Clark Five	Bits and pieces	2	11-Mar
Brian Poole & The Tremeloes	Candy man	6	11-Mar
Freddie & The Dreamers	Over you	13	11-Mar
Roy Orbison	Borne on the wind	15	18-Mar
Kathy Kirby	Let me go, lover	10	18-Mar
Dusty Springfield	Stay awhile	13	18-Mar
Eden Kane	Boys cry	8	25-Mar
Billy J. Kramer & The Dakotas	Little children	1	25-Mar
Jim Reeves	I love you because	5	01-Apr
Hollies	Just one look	2	01-Apr
Rolling Stones	Not fade away	3	01-Apr
Gene Pitney	That girl belongs to yesterday	7	01-Apr
Beatles	Can't buy me love	1	08-Apr
Shadows	Theme for young lovers	12	15-Apr
Elvis Presley	Viva Las Vegas	17	15-Apr
Swinging Blue Jeans	Good golly Miss Molly	11	22-Apr
Applejacks	Tell me when	7	22-Apr

Artist	Title	Pos	Date
Peter & Gordon	A world without love	1	29-Apr
Mojos	Everything's alright	9	06-May
Manfred Mann	Hubble bubble (toil and trouble)	11	06-May
Migil 5	Mockin' Bird Hill	10	06-May
Doris Day	Move over darling	8	06-May
Gerry & The Pacemakers	Don't let the sun catch you crying	6	13-May
Searchers	Don't throw your love away	1	13-May
Merseybeats	Don't turn around	13	13-May
Bachelors	I believe	2	13-May
Richard Anthony	If I loved you	18	13-May
Dionne Warwick	Walk on by	9	13-May
Billy Fury	I will	14	27-May
Four Pennies	Juliet	1	27-May
Millie	My boy lollipop	2	27-May
Fourmost	A little loving	6	03-Jun
Cilla Black	You're my world	1	03-Jun
Kathy Kirby	You're the one	17	03-Jun
Cliff Richard	Constantly	4	10-Jun
Shadows	The rise and fall of Flingel Bunt	5	10-Jun
Freddie & The Dreamers	I love you baby	16	17-Jun
Chuck Berry	No particluar place to go	3	17-Jun
Gigliola Cinquetti	Non ho l'eta per amarti	17	17-Jun
Hollies	Here I go again	4	24-Jun
Mary Wells	My guy	5	24-Jun
Lulu & The Luvvers	Shout	7	24-Jun
Little Richard	Bama lama bama loo	20	01-Jul
Dave Clark Five	Can't you see that she's mine	10	01-Jul
Louis Armstrong	Hello, Dolly!	4	01-Jul
Frankie Vaughan	Hello, Dolly!	18	01-Jul
Roy Orbison	It's over	1	01-Jul
Brian Poole & The Tremeloes	Someone, someone	2	01-Jul
Applejacks	Like dreamers do	20	08-Jul

Peter & Gordon	Nobody I know	10	08-Jul
Bachelors	Ramona	4	08-Jul
Swinging Blue Jeans	You're no good	3	08-Jul
P.J.Proby	Hold me	3	15-Jul
Animals	House of the rising sun	1	15-Jul
Elvis Presley	Kissin' cousins	10	15-Jul
Rolling Stones	It's all over now	1	22-Jul
Beatles	A hard day's night	1	29-Jul
Dusty Springfield	I just don't know what to do with myself	3	29-Jul
Merseybeats	Wishin' and hopin'	13	05-Aug
Barron Knights	Call up the groups (medley)	3	12-Aug
Cliff Richard	On the beach	7	12-Aug
Searchers	Some day we're gonna love again	11	12-Aug
Nashville Teens	Tobacco Road	6	12-Aug
Manfred Mann	Do wah diddy diddy	1	19-Aug
Four Pennies	I found out the hard way	14	19-Aug
Billy Fury	It's only make believe	10	19-Aug
Dionne Warwick	You'll never get to heaven (if you break my heart)	20	19-Aug
Billy J.Kramer & The Dakotas	From a window	10	26-Aug
Honeycombs	Have I the right?	1	02-Sep
Beach Boys	I get around	7	02-Sep
Jim Reeves	I won't forget you	3	02-Sep
Cilla Black	It's for you	7	09-Sep
Elvis Presley	Such a night	13	09-Sep
Dave Berry	The crying game	5	09-Sep
Marianne Faithfull	As tears go by	9	16-Sep
Bachelors	I wouldn't trade you for the world	4	16-Sep
Zombies	She's not there	12	16-Sep
Kinks	You really got me	1	16-Sep
Herman's Hermits	I'm into something good	1	30-Sep
Brenda Lee	Is it true?	17	30-Sep

Artist	Title		Date
Four Seasons	Rag doll	2	30-Sep
Roy Orbison	Oh pretty woman	1	07-Oct
Supremes	Where did our love go?	3	07-Oct
Newbeats	Bread and butter	15	14-Oct
Dean Martin	Everybody loves somebody sometime	11	14-Oct
P.J.Proby	Together	8	14-Oct
Animals	I'm crying	8	21-Oct
Sandie Shaw	(There's) always something there to remind me	1	28-Oct
Henry Mancini & His Orchestra	How soon	10	28-Oct
Lesley Gore	Maybe I know	20	28-Oct
Searchers	When you walk in the room	3	28-Oct
Cliff Bennett & The Rebel Rousers	One way love	9	04-Nov
Cliff Richard	The twelfth of never	8	04-Nov
Julie Rogers	The wedding	3	04-Nov
Hollies	We're through	7	04-Nov
Matt Monro	Walk away	4	11-Nov
Elvis Presley	Ain't that lovin' you baby	15	18-Nov
Nashville Teens	Google eye	10	18-Nov
Manfred Mann	Sha la la	3	18-Nov
Kinks	All day and all of the night	2	25-Nov
Supremes	Baby love	1	25-Nov
Pretty Things	Don't bring me down	10	25-Nov
Rockin' Berries	He's in town	3	25-Nov
Shangri-La's	Remember (walkin' in the sand)	14	25-Nov
Helmut Zacharias	Tokyo melody	9	25-Nov
Four Pennies	Black girl	20	02-Dec
Wayne Fontana & The Mindbenders	Um, um, um, um, um, um	5	02-Dec
Gene Pitney	I'm gonna be strong	2	09-Dec
Rolling Stones	Little red rooster	1	09-Dec
Dusty Springfield	Losing you	9	09-Dec
Herman's Hermits	Show me girl	19	09-Dec

Artist	Song	Position	Date
Beatles	I feel fine	1	16-Dec
Jim Reeves	There's a heartache following me	6	16-Dec
Petula Clark	Downtown	2	23-Dec
Adam Faith	A message to Martha (Kentucky Bluebird)	12	23-Dec
Cliff Richard	I could easily fall	9	23-Dec
Roy Orbison	Pretty paper	6	23-Dec
Val Doonican	Walk tall	3	23-Dec
Elvis Presley	Blue Christmas	11	30-Dec
Sandie Shaw	Girl don't come	13	30-Dec
Freddie & The Dreamers	I understand	5	30-Dec
Bachelors	No arms could ever hold you	7	30-Dec
P.J.Proby	Somewhere	10	30-Dec
Twinkle	Terry	12	30-Dec
Searchers	What have they done to the rain?	16	30-Dec
Georgie Fame	Yeh yeh	17	30-Dec

The events ....

- Southampton was granted city status[65]
- The Queen gave birth to her fourth child and third son, Edward, Earl of Wessex[73]
- Violent disturbances took place between Mods & Rockers at Clacton Beach in Essex[66]
- The National Trust re-opened the southern section of the Stratford-upon-Avon Canal, the first major restoration of a canal for leisure use[67]

Mods
© *Sergio Calleja (2006) /*
Wikimedia Commons / CC BY-SA
2.0 Generic

Rockers
© *Triton Rocker (2010) /*
Wikimedia Commons /
CC BY-SA 3.0 Unported

- The Forth Road Bridge was opened over the Firth of Forth, linking Fife and Edinburgh[70]

Forth Road Bridge
© *Klaus with K (2002) / Wikimedia Commons / CC BY-SA 3.0 Unported*

In the world of sport ......

- Great Britain and Northern Ireland competed at the Winter Olympics in Innsbruck, Austria and won one gold medal[73]
- Liverpool FC won the Football League First Division title for the sixth time[68]
- West Ham United took the FA Cup with a 3-2 win over Preston North End at Wembley Stadium[73]
- Great Britain competed at the Summer Olympics in Tokyo and won 4 gold, 12 silver and 2 bronze medals[73]
- Donald Campbell set the world speed record on water at 276.33 mph in Australia[70]

In the world of entertainment.......

- Teen girls' magazine *'Jackie'* was first published[69]
- Actor Peter Sellers married actress Britt Ekland[73]
- Pirate radio stations Radio Caroline and Radio Atlanta began broadcasting[70]
- BBC Two began broadcasting with its first program *'Play School'*[70]
- Pirate radio station Radio Sutch began broadcasting from Shivering Sands Army Fort in the Thames Estuary[71]
- The Beatles film, 'A Hard Day's *Night'* was released[72]
- The first broadcast of the BBC's *'Match of the Day'* took place on BBC Two[73]
- ITV launched its soap opera *'Crossroads'*[70]
- Pirate radio station Wonderful Radio London began broadcasting from MV *Galaxy* anchored off Frinton-on-Sea, with a Fab 40 playlist of popular

Britt Ekland & Peter Sellers
Credit: sydsvenskan.se (1964) / Wikimedia Commons / Public Domain

- records[73]
- Ian Fleming's James Bond novel *'You Only Live Twice'* was published[73]
- The first broadcast of the BBC's *'Top Of The Pops'* took place[73]
- The Beatles toured the US and a crowd of some 150,000 people welcomed them back to Liverpool[73]
- John Lennon's first book, *'In His Own Write'*, was published[73]
- Peter & Gordon released their first single, *'A World Without Love'*, a Paul McCartney song that McCartney decided was not good enough for The Beatles. The song ultimately topped the UK and US charts[74]
- Drummer Keith Moon joined The Who[74]
- The Rolling Stones released their debut album[74]
- The Rolling Stones performed 2 tours of the US[74]
- The UK finished second in the Eurovision Song Contest with ' I Love the Little Things' sung by Matt Monro[74]

Peter & Gordon
Credit: General Artists Corporation (1965) / Wikimedia Commons / Public Domain

In the world of business.....

- The British and French governments agreed a deal for the construction of the Channel Tunnel[75]
- £10 bank notes were issued for the first time since the Second World War[73]
- The first portable television went on sale[73]
- The first Habitat store was opened in London's Fulham Road[70]
- The UK's first undercover shopping centre, The Bull Ring, was officially open in Birmingham, England[76]
- The construction of the Post Office Tower in London was completed[66]
- *'The Sun'* newspaper went into circulation, replacing the *Daily Herald*[73]
- The Hanson Trust was established by James Hanson and Gordon White to purchase Under-performing companies and turn them around[77]

Post Office Tower (BT Tower)
Credit: David Castor (2009) / Wikimedia Commons / Public Domain

In the world of transport.....

- The British Motor Corporation launched the Austin 1800 which was to become European Car of the Year[73]
- It was announced that the American car manufacturer Chrysler was taking a substantial share in the British Rootes Group, which included the Hillman, Singer and Sunbeam marques[78]
- Daihatsu became the first Japanese carmaker to import passenger cars into the United Kingdom[79]

Austin 1800
© *DeFacto (2006) / Wikimedia Commons / CC BY-SA 2.5*

1965

Welcome to the lighter side of life in Britain in 1965

The music ……

Artist	Title	Highest position this year	W/E date
Adam Faith	A message to Martha (Kentucky Bluebird)	12	06-Jan
Supremes	Baby love	18	06-Jan
Elvis Presley	Blue Christmas	15	06-Jan
Petula Clark	Downtown	2	06-Jan
Cliff Richard	I could easily fall	6	06-Jan
Beatles	I feel fine	1	06-Jan
Freddie & The Dreamers	I understand	5	06-Jan
Gene Pitney	I'm gonna be strong	4	06-Jan
Julie Rogers	Like a child	20	06-Jan
Rolling Stones	Little red rooster	14	06-Jan
Bachelors	No arms could ever hold you	8	06-Jan
Roy Orbison	Pretty paper	13	06-Jan
Val Doonican	Walk tall	3	06-Jan
Kinks	All day and all of the night	19	13-Jan
Twinkle	Terry	4	13-Jan
Jim Reeves	There's a heartache following me	18	13-Jan
Searchers	What have they done to the rain?	13	13-Jan
Shadows	Genie with the light brown lamp	17	20-Jan
P.J.Proby	Somewhere	6	20-Jan
Georgie Fame	Yeh yeh	1	20-Jan
Sounds Orchestral	Cast your fate to the wind	5	27-Jan
Gerry & The Paceakers	Ferry 'cross the Mersey	8	27-Jan

Artist	Title		Date
Sandie Shaw	Girl don't come	3	27-Jan
Moody Blues	Go now	1	03-Feb
Brian Poole & The Tremeloes	Three bells	17	03-Feb
Cilla Black	You've lost that lovin' feelin'	2	03-Feb
Manfred Mann	Come tomorrow	4	10-Feb
Billy Fury	I'm lost without you	16	10-Feb
Righteous Brothers	You've lost that lovin' feelin'	1	10-Feb
Them	Baby please don't go	10	17-Feb
Del Shannon	Keep searchin' (we'll follow the sun)	3	17-Feb
Shangri-La's	Leader of the pack	11	17-Feb
Val Doonican	The special years	7	17-Feb
Kinks	Tired of waiting for you	1	24-Feb
Animals	Don't let me be misunderstood	3	03-Mar
Roy Orbison	Goodnight	14	03-Mar
Seekers	I'll never find another you	1	03-Mar
Jim Reeves	It hurts so much (to see you go)	8	03-Mar
Wayne Fontana & The Mindbenders	The game of love	2	03-Mar
Ivy League	Funny how love can be	8	10-Mar
Gene Pitney	I must be seeing things	6	10-Mar
Shadows	Mary Anne	17	10-Mar
Sandie Shaw	I'll stop at nothing	4	17-Mar
Tom Jones	It's not unusual	1	17-Mar
Herman's Hermits	Silhouettes	3	17-Mar
Elvis Presley	Do the clam	19	24-Mar
Pretty Things	Honey I need	13	24-Mar
P.J.Proby	I apologize	11	24-Mar
Rolling Stones	The last time	1	24-Mar
Hollies	Yes I will	9	24-Mar
Marianne Faithfull	Come and stay with me	4	31-Mar
Petula Clark	I know a place	17	31-Mar

Artist	Song	#	Date
Searchers	Goodbye my love	4	07-Apr
Unit Four Plus Two	Concrete and clay	1	14-Apr
Yardbirds	For your love	3	14-Apr
Keely Smith	You're breakin' my heart	14	14-Apr
Donovan	Catch the wind	4	21-Apr
The Who	I can't explain	8	21-Apr
Gerry & The Paceakers	I'll be there	15	21-Apr
Supremes	Stop! In the name of love	7	21-Apr
Cliff Richard	The minute you're gone	1	21-Apr
Bob Dylan	The times they are a changin'	9	21-Apr
Kinks	Everybody's gonna be happy	17	28-Apr
Them	Here comes the night	2	28-Apr
Dave Berry	Little things	5	28-Apr
Beatles	Ticket to ride	1	28-Apr
Animals	Bring it on home to me	7	05-May
Barron Knights	Pop go the workers	5	05-May
Manfred Mann	Oh no not my baby	11	12-May
Seekers	A world of our own	3	19-May
Cilla Black	I've been wrong before	17	19-May
Roger Miller	King of the road	1	19-May
Bob Dylan	Subterranean homesick blues	9	26-May
Marianne Faithfull	This little bird	6	26-May
Peter & Gordon	True love ways	2	26-May
Jackie Trent	Where are you now (my love)	1	26-May
Herman's Hermits	Wonderful world	7	26-May
Sandie Shaw	Long live love	1	02-Jun
Francoise Hardy	All over the world	16	09-Jun
Jim Reeves	Not until the next time	13	09-Jun
Rockin' Berries	Poor man's son	5	09-Jun
Billy J.Kramer & The Dakotas	Trains and boats and planes	12	16-Jun
Elvis Presley	Crying in the chapel	1	23-Jun

Walker Brothers	Love her	20	23-Jun
Bachelors	Marie	9	23-Jun
Everly Brothers	The price of love	2	23-Jun
Unit Four Plus Two	(You've) never been in love like this before	14	30-Jun
Dave Clark Five	Come home	16	30-Jun
Hollies	I'm alive	1	30-Jun
Kinks	Set me free	9	30-Jun
Shadows	Stingray	19	30-Jun
Shirley Ellis	The clapping song	6	30-Jun
Burt Bacharach	Trains and boats and planes	4	30-Jun
The Who	Anyway, anyhow, anywhere	10	07-Jul
Donovan	Colours	4	07-Jul
Cliff Richard	On my word	12	07-Jul
Wayne Fontana & The Mindbenders	Just a little bit too late	20	14-Jul
Gene Pitney	Looking through the eyes of love	3	14-Jul
Peter & Gordon	To know you is to love you	5	14-Jul
Yardbirds	Heart full of soul	2	21-Jul
Lulu	Leave a little love	8	21-Jul
Sir Douglas Quintet	She's about a mover	15	21-Jul
Byrds	Mr.Tambourine man	1	28-Jul
Ivy League	Tossing and turning	3	28-Jul
Peter Cook & Dudley Moore	Goodbye-ee	18	04-Aug
Dusty Springfield	In the middle of nowhere	8	04-Aug
P.J.Proby	Let the water run down	19	04-Aug
Beatles	Help!	1	11-Aug
Searchers	He's got no love	12	11-Aug
Joan Baez	There but for fortune	8	11-Aug
Tom Jones	With these hands	13	11-Aug
Sam The Sham & The Pharoahs	Wooly bully	11	11-Aug
Dave Clark Five	Catch us if you can	5	18-Aug
Billy Fury	In thoughts of you	9	18-Aug

Artist	Title		Date
Marianne Faithfull	Summer nights	10	18-Aug
Animals	We gotta get out of this place	2	18-Aug
Fortunes	You've got your troubles	2	25-Aug
Shadows	Don't make my baby blue	10	01-Sep
Jonathan King	Everyone's gone to the moon	4	01-Sep
Sonny & Cher	I got you babe	1	01-Sep
Horst Jankowski	Walk in the Black Forest	3	01-Sep
Byrds	All I really want to do	4	08-Sep
Kinks	See my friend	10	08-Sep
Tom Jones	What's new pussycat?	11	08-Sep
Marcello Minerbi	Zorba's dance	6	08-Sep
Rolling Stones	(I can't get no) Satisfaction	1	15-Sep
Cher	All I really want to do	9	15-Sep
Righteous Brothers	Unchained melody	14	15-Sep
Sonny	Laugh at me	9	22-Sep
Bob Dylan	Like a rolling stone	4	22-Sep
Herman's Hermits	Just a little bit better	15	29-Sep
Walker Brothers	Make it easy on yourself	1	29-Sep
Honeycombs	That's the way	12	29-Sep
Ken Dodd	Tears	1	06-Oct
Hollies	Look through any window	4	06-Oct
Sonny & Cher	Baby don't go	11	13-Oct
Manfred Mann	If you gotta go, go now	2	13-Oct
Andy Williams	Almost there	2	20-Oct
McCoys	Hang on Sloopy	5	20-Oct
Nino Rosso	Il silenzio	8	20-Oct
Small Faces	Whatcha gonna do about it	14	20-Oct
Wilson Pickett	In the midnight hour	12	27-Oct
Sandie Shaw	Message understood	6	27-Oct

Artist	Title		Date
Dusty Springfield	Some of your lovin'	8	27-Oct
Barry McGuire	Eve of destruction	3	03-Nov
Sonny & Cher	But you're mine	17	10-Nov
Yardbirds	Evil hearted you / Still I'm sad	3	10-Nov
Rolling Stones	Get off of my cloud	1	10-Nov
Hedgehoppers Anonymous	It's good news week	5	10-Nov
Matt Monro	Yesterday	8	10-Nov
Peter & Gordon	Baby I'm yours	19	17-Nov
Fortunes	Here it comes again	4	17-Nov
Animals	It's my life	7	17-Nov
Everly Brothers	Love is strange	11	17-Nov
Chris Andrews	Yesterday man	3	17-Nov
Four Pennies	Until it's time for you to go	19	24-Nov
The Who	My generation	2	01-Dec
Seekers	The carnival is over	1	01-Dec
Len Barry	1,2,3	3	08-Dec
Toys	A lover's concerto	5	08-Dec
Roy Orbison	Crawlin' back	19	08-Dec
Paul & Barry Ryan	Don't bring me your heartaches	13	08-Dec
Jim Reeves	Is it really over	17	08-Dec
Bob Dylan	Positively 4th Street	8	08-Dec
Gene Pitney	Princess in rags	9	08-Dec
Elvis Presley	Tell me why	15	08-Dec
P.J.Proby	Maria	8	22-Dec
Beatles	Day tripper / We can work it out	1	22-Dec
Fontella Bass	Rescue me	11	22-Dec
Spencer Davis Group	Keep on running	15	29-Dec
Four Seasons	Let's hang on	10	29-Dec
Barron Knights	Merry gentle pops	19	29-Dec
Walker Brothers	My ship is coming in	6	29-Dec
Ken Dodd	The river	3	29-Dec
Kinks	Till the end of the day	14	29-Dec
Chris Andrews	To whom it concerns	13	29-Dec
Shadows	War Lord	18	29-Dec
Cliff Richard	Wind me up (let me go)	2	29-Dec

The events ……....

- Goldie, a London Zoo golden eagle, was recaptured after 13 days of freedom[80]
- The 700th anniversary of Parliament was celebrated[81]
- Elizabeth Lane was appointed as the first female High Court judge, assigned to the Family Division[81]

In the world of sport ……

- Sir Stanley Matthews played his final First Division football game, at the record age of 50 years and 5 days[81]
- Manchester United won the Football League First Division title[82]
- Liverpool FC won the FA Cup for the first time with a 2-1 win over Leeds United at Wembley[81]
- West Ham United beat 1860 Munich 2-0 at Wembley Stadium to win the European Cup Winners Cup[81]
- Charlton Athletic F.C. player Keith Peacock became the first substitute to appear in a Football League match[83]

In the world of entertainment……..

- The Beatles film *'Help!'*, debuted in London[93]
- The first episode of *'Thunderbirds'* was broadcast on ATV[81]
- Men's magazine *Mayfair* was first published[81]
- The Beatles' last live UK tour concluded with two performances at the Capitol, Cardiff[84]
- Ian Fleming's James Bond novel *'The Man With The Golden Gun'* was published[81]
- Charlie Watts' book – *'Ode To A Flying Bird'* – a tribute to jazz great Charlie Parker was published[85]

Kathy Kirby
Credit: RAI (1965) / Wikimedia Commons / Public Domain

- Paul Simon broadcasted on BBC radio for the first time on the *Five to Ten* show[85]
- Kathy Kirby finished second in the 10th Eurovision Song Contest in Naples, Italy with the song "*I Belong*"[85]
- Alan Price left The Animals due to his fear of flying[85]
- The Beatles were appointed Members of the British Empire (MBE) by the Queen[85]
- The Beatles received a record 5 Ivor Novello awards[86]
- The Beatles visited Elvis at his home in Bel-Air – the only time that the band and the singer met[85]
- The film *Catch Us If You Can,* starring the Dave Clark Five, was released[85]

- The film *Every Day's a Holiday,* starring John Leyton, Michael Sarne and Peter Birrell, was released[85]

The Beatles
Credit: United Press Int'l
(1964) / Wikimedia Commons /
Public Domain

Dave Clark Five
Credit: MGM (1964) / Wikimedia Commons
/ Public Domain

- The film *Three Hats for Lisa,* starring Joe Brown, Sid James and Una Stubbs, was released[85]
- The film *Up Jumped a Swagman,* starring Frank Ifield, Annette Andre and Suzy Kendall, was released[85]

In the world of business.....

- Corgi Toys introduced the all-time best-selling model car, James Bond's Aston Martin DB5 from the film *Goldfinger*[87]
- The Post Office Tower opened in London[93]
- Mary Quant introduced the miniskirt from her shop *'Bazaar'* on the Kings Road in Chelsea, London[88,89,90]
- Asda opened its first supermarket in Castleford, Yorkshire[91]
- The Rotunda landmark office building was completed in Birmingham city centre[81]

Aston Martin DB 5
Credit: Martin Hidinger (2003)
/ Wikimedia Commons / Public Domain

In the world of education.....

- The Secretary of State for Education and Science issued instructions for local authorities to convert their schools to the Comprehensive system[92]
- The Certificate of Secondary Education (CSE) was introduced as a school-leaving qualification in England, Wales and Northern Ireland[81]

In the world of transport.....

- The Pennine Way was officially opened[93]
- A 70mph speed limit was imposed on British roads[93]
- The motorway network continued to expand with additional sections of the M6, M4, A1, M1, M5, M8 and M2 all being opened[81]
- Toyota began importing passenger cars to the United Kingdom when the Corona model was launched[81]

Toyota Corona
© *Mytho88 (2008) / Wikimedia Commons / CC BY-SA 3.0 Unported*

The Rotunda
© *Erebus 555(2007) / Wikimedia Commons / CC BY-SA 3.0 Unported*

1966

Welcome to the lighter side of life in Britain in 1966

The music ……

Artist	Title	Highest position this year	W/E date
Len Barry	1,2,3	8	05-Jan
Toys	A lovers concerto	9	05-Jan
Beatles	Day tripper / We can work it out	1	05-Jan
P.J.Proby	Maria	12	05-Jan
The Who	My generation	7	05-Jan
Bob Dylan	Positively 4th Street	17	05-Jan
Gene Pitney	Princess in rags	16	05-Jan
Fontella Bass	Rescue me	11	05-Jan
Ken Dodd	Tears	5	05-Jan
Ken Dodd	The river	3	05-Jan
Chris Andrews	To whom it concerns	13	05-Jan
Shadows	War Lord	18	05-Jan
Cliff Richard	Wind me up (let me go)	2	05-Jan
Chris Andrews	Yesterday man	20	05-Jan
Barron Knights	Merry gentle pops	9	12-Jan
Seekers	The carnival is over	3	12-Jan
Hollies	If I needed someone	20	19-Jan
Kinks	Till the end of the day	8	19-Jan
Peter Sellers	A hard day's night	14	26-Jan
Spencer Davis Group	Keep on running	1	26-Jan
Four Seasons	Let's hang on	4	26-Jan
Walker Brothers	My ship is coming in	3	26-Jan
Searchers	Take me for what I'm worth	20	26-Jan
Vince Hill	Take me to your heart again	13	26-Jan
Herman's Hermits	A must to avoid	6	02-Feb

Artist	Title		
Bob Dylan	Can you please crawl out your window?	17	02-Feb
Roger Miller	England swings	13	02-Feb
Overlanders	Michelle	1	02-Feb
Otis Redding	My girl	11	02-Feb
Herb Alpert & The Tijuana Brass	Spanish flea	3	02-Feb
Cilla Black	Love's just a broken heart	5	09-Feb
David & Jonathan	Michelle	11	09-Feb
St.Louis Union	Girl	11	16-Feb
Paul & Barry Ryan	Have pity on the boy	18	16-Feb
Len Barry	Like a baby	10	16-Feb
Pinkerton's Assorted Colours	Mirror, mirror	9	16-Feb
Crispian St.Peters	You were on my mind	2	16-Feb
Rolling Stones	19th nervous breakdown	2	23-Feb
Dusty Springfield	Little by little	17	23-Feb
Barbra Streisand	Second hand Rose	14	23-Feb
Nancy Sinatra	These boots are made for walkin'	1	23-Feb
Sandie Shaw	Tomorrow	9	23-Feb
Animals	Inside - looking out	12	09-Mar
Petula Clark	My love	4	09-Mar
Stevie Wonder	Uptight (everything's alright)	14	09-Mar
Mindbenders	A groovy kind of love	2	16-Mar
Gene Pitney	Backstage	4	16-Mar
Beach Boys	Barbara Ann	3	16-Mar
Fortunes	This golden ring	15	16-Mar
Hollies	I can't let go	2	23-Mar
Lou Christie	Lightning strikes	11	23-Mar
Andy Williams	May each day	19	23-Mar
Walker Brothers	The sun ain't gonna shine anymore	1	23-Mar
Small Faces	Sha la la la lee	3	23-Mar
Yardbirds	Shapes of things	3	30-Mar
Sonny & Cher	What now my love	13	30-Mar
Bob Lind	Elusive butterfly	5	06-Apr

Artist	Title	Pos	Date
Kinks	Dedicated follower of fashion	4	06-Apr
Eddy Arnold	Make the world go away	8	06-Apr
Cliff Richard	Blue turns to grey	15	13-Apr
Dave Dee, Dozy, Beaky Mick & Tich	Hold tight!	4	20-Apr
Spencer Davis Group	Somebody help me	1	20-Apr
Seekers	Someday one day	11	20-Apr
Bachelors	Sound of silence	3	20-Apr
The Who	Substitute	5	20-Apr
Herman's Hermits	You won't be leavin'	20	20-Apr
Val Doonican	Elusive butterfly	5	27-Apr
Alan Price Set	I put a spell on you	9	27-Apr
Graham Bonney	Supergirl	19	04-May
Dusty Springfield	You don't have to say you love me	1	04-May
Cilla Black	Alfie	9	11-May
Cher	Bang bang (my baby shot me down)	3	11-May
Lovin' Spoonful	Daydream	2	11-May
Manfred Mann	Pretty flamingo	1	11-May
Righteous Brothers	(You're my) Soul and inspiration	15	18-May
Simon & Garfunkel	Homeward bound	9	18-May
Nancy Sinatra	How does that grab you darlin'	19	18-May
Neil Christian	That's nice	14	18-May
Crispian St.Peters	The Pied Piper	5	18-May
Roy 'C'	Shotgun wedding	6	25-May
Beach Boys	Sloop John B	2	25-May
Small Faces	Hey girl	10	01-Jun
Rolling Stones	Paint it black	1	01-Jun
Troggs	Wild thing	2	01-Jun
Sandie Shaw	Nothing come easy	14	08-Jun
Bob Dylan	Rainy day women no's 12 and 35	7	08-Jun
Merseys	Sorrow	4	08-Jun
Frank Sinatra	Strangers in the night	1	08-Jun
Wayne Fontana	Come on home	16	15-Jun
Paul & Barry Ryan	I love her	17	15-Jun

Tom Jones	Once there was a time / Not responsible	18	15-Jun
Ken Dodd	Promises	6	15-Jun
Mamas & Papas	Monday Monday	3	22-Jun
Yardbirds	Over under sideways down	10	22-Jun
Animals	Don't bring me down	6	29-Jun
Four Seasons	Opus 17 (Don't you worry 'bout me)	20	29-Jun
Beatles	Paperback writer	1	29-Jun
Percy Sledge	When a man loves a woman	4	29-Jun
Cilla Black	Don't answer me	6	06-Jul
Dave Dee, Dozy, Beaky Mick & Tich	Hideaway	10	06-Jul
Simon & Garfunkel	I am a rock	17	06-Jul
James Brown	It's a man's man's man's world	13	13-Jul
Roy Orbison	Lana	15	13-Jul
Ike & Tina Turner	River deep, mountain high	3	13-Jul
Kinks	Sunny afternoon	1	13-Jul
Herman's Hermits	This door swings both ways	18	13-Jul
Hollies	Bus stop	5	20-Jul
Gene Pitney	Nobody needs your love	2	20-Jul
Georgie Fame & The Blue Flames	Getaway	1	27-Jul
Walker Brothers	(Baby) You don't have to tell me	13	03-Aug
Los Bravos	Black is black	2	03-Aug
Dusty Springfield	Going back	10	03-Aug
Petula Clark	I couldn't live without your love	6	03-Aug
Chris Farlowe	Out of time	1	03-Aug
Elvis Presley	Love letters	6	10-Aug
Troggs	With a girl like you	1	10-Aug
Bob Dylan	I want you	16	17-Aug
Chris Montez	The more I see you	3	17-Aug
Dave Berry	Mama	5	24-Aug

Lovin' Spoonful	Summer in the city	8	24-Aug
Cliff Richard	Visions	7	24-Aug
Beatles	Yellow submarine / Eleanor Rigby	1	24-Aug
Beach Boys	God only knows	2	31-Aug
Alan Price Set	Hi-lili, hi-lo	11	31-Aug
Ken Dodd	More than love	14	31-Aug
Napoleon XIV	They're coming to take me away, ha ha!	4	31-Aug
Mamas & Papas	I saw her again	11	07-Sep
David & Jonathan	Lovers of the world unite	7	14-Sep
Small Faces	All or nothing	1	21-Sep
Cliff Bennett & The Rebel Rousers	Got to get you into my life	6	21-Sep
Manfred Mann	Just like a woman	10	21-Sep
Lee Dorsey	Working in the coal mine	8	21-Sep
Mindbenders	Ashes to ashes	14	28-Sep
Jim Reeves	Distant drums	1	28-Sep
Roy Orbison	Too soon to know	3	28-Sep
Spencer Davis Group	When I come home	12	28-Sep
The Who	I'm a boy	2	05-Oct
Sonny & Cher	Little man	4	05-Oct
Seekers	Walk with me	10	05-Oct
Supremes	You can't hurry love	3	05-Oct
Dusty Springfield	All I see is you	9	12-Oct
Dave Dee, Dozy, Beaky Mick & Tich	Bend it!	2	12-Oct
Los Bravos	I don't care	16	12-Oct
Bobby Hebb	Sunny	12	12-Oct
Walker Brothers	Another tear falls	12	19-Oct
Sandpipers	Guantanamera	7	19-Oct
Rolling Stones	Have you seen you mother, baby, standing in the shadow?	5	19-Oct
Peter & Gordon	Lady Godiva	16	19-Oct
Georgie Fame	Sunny	13	19-Oct
New Vaudeville Band	Winchester Cathedral	4	19-Oct
Troggs	I can't control myself	2	02-Nov

Artist	Title	Weeks	Date
Four Tops	Reach out I'll be there	1	02-Nov
Elvis Presley	All that I am	18	09-Nov
Four Seasons	I've got you under my skin	12	09-Nov
Herman's Hermits	No milk today	7	09-Nov
Hollies	Stop stop stop	2	09-Nov
Cliff Richard	Time drags by	10	09-Nov
Temptations	Beauty is only skin deep	18	16-Nov
Paul Jones	High time	4	16-Nov
Cilla Black	A fool am I	13	23-Nov
Beach Boys	Good vibrations	1	23-Nov
Lee Dorsey	Holy cow	6	23-Nov
Bobby Darin	If I were a carpenter	9	23-Nov
Manfred Mann	Semi-detached suburban Mr. James	2	23-Nov
Ike & Tina Turner	A love like yours	16	30-Nov
Spencer Davis Group	Gimme some loving	2	30-Nov
Eric Burdon & The Animals	Help me girl	14	30-Nov
Tom Jones	Green, green grass of home	1	07-Dec
Gene Pitney	Just one smile	8	14-Dec
Small Faces	My mind's eye	4	14-Dec
Easybeats	Friday on my mind	6	21-Dec
Jimmy Ruffin	What becomes of the broken-hearted?	10	21-Dec
Val Doonican	What would I be?	2	21-Dec
Kinks	Dead end street	5	28-Dec
The Who	Happy Jack	17	28-Dec
Elvis Presley	If every day was like Christmas	13	28-Dec
Seekers	Morningtown ride	2	28-Dec
Dave Dee, Dozy, Beaky Mick & Tich	Save me	6	28-Dec
Roy Orbison	There won't be many coming home	18	28-Dec
Barron Knights	Under new management	20	28-Dec
Supremes	You keep me hangin' on	8	28-Dec

| Donovan | Sunshine Superman | 4 | 28-Dec |

The events ....

- Longleat Safari Park, the first drive-through wildlife park outside of Africa, was opened[99]

In the world of sport ......

- The football world cup was stolen whilst on exhibition in London and later found in a South London garden wrapped in a newspaper by a mongrel dog called Pickles[94]
- Liverpool FC won the Football League First Division title for the second time[95]
- Everton defeated Sheffield Wednesday 3-2 in the FA Cup final at Wembley Stadium[99]
- England beat West Germany 4-2 to win the World Cup at Wembley in a game which attracted an all-time record UK television audience of over 32 million[96],[97]
- Everton signed Alan Ball from Blackpool for a national record fee of £110,000[98]

Jules Rimet Trophy
© *Sailko (2014) Wikimedia Commons / CC BY-SA 3.0 Unported*

In the world of entertainment.......

- Children's series *'Camberwick Green'* was first broadcast on BBC1[99]
- Radio Caroline South pirate radio ship MV Mi Amigo ran aground on the beach at Frinton[99]
- The BBC1 sitcom *'Till Death Us Do Part'* was first broadcast[99]
- The soft-porn magazine *Fiesta* was first published[99]
- Swinging Radio England and Britain Radio began broadcasting on the AM waveband from the same ship anchored off the South coast of England in international waters[99]
- Ian Fleming's James Bond novels *'Octopussy'* and *'The Living Daylights'* were published[99]
- Young singer David Jones changed his name to David Bowie to avoid confusion with the Monkees front man Davy Jones[100]
- The UK's Kenneth McKellar, singing "A Man Without Love", finished 9th in the Eurovision Song Contest[100]
- The *Disc Weekly* publication was incorporated with *Music Echo* magazine[100]
- The musical film *Dateline Diamonds,* starring The Small Faces, was released[100]

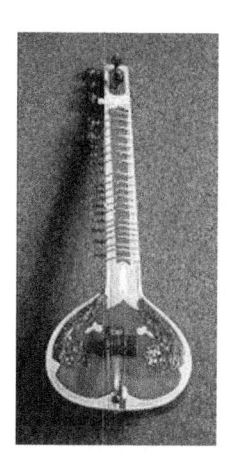

Sitar
Credit: Jan Kraus (2008) Wikimedia Commons / Publilc Domain

59

- The Rolling Stones track *'Paint It Black'* was the first UK and US number 1 hit to feature a Sitar (in this case played by Brian Jones)[100]
- John Lennon met Yoko Ono when attending a preview of her art exhibition in London[101]

The Small Faces
Credit: Press Records (1965) / Wikimedia Commons / Public Domain

Herman's Hermits
Credit: NBC Television (1968) Wikimedia Commons / Public Domain

Spencer Davis Group
© Ron Kroon (1966) / Wikimedia Commons / CC BY-SA 3.0 Unported

- The musical film *Finders Keepers,* starring Cliff Richard, was released[100]
- The musical film *Hold On!* Starring Herman's Hermits, was released[100]
- The musical film *The Ghost Goes Gear,* starring the Spencer Davis Group, was released[100]

In the world of business…..

- Barclays Bank introduced the Barclaycard, the first British credit card[102]

In the world of transport…..

- The first cross channel hovercraft service from Ramsgate to Calais was inaugurated[99]
- The MK2 Ford Cortina was launched[103]

Ford Cortina Mk II
© Brian Snelson (2008) / Wikimedia Commons / CC BY 2.0 Generic

Hillman Hunter
© Charles01 (2009) / Wikimedia Commons / CC BY-SA 3.0 Unported

- The Rootes Group launched the Hillman Hunter to compete with the Austin 1800, Ford Cortina and Vauxhall Victor[99]
- The motorway network continued to expand with extensions to the M1, M4, M6, and the new M32 and M74 being opened[99]
- Japanese car manufacturer Nissan began importing its range of Datsun branded cars to the United Kingdom[99]

1967

Welcome to the lighter side of life in Britain in 1967

The music ……

Artist	Title	Highest position this year	W/E date
Kinks	Dead end street	5	04-Jan
Jim Reeves	Distant drums	16	04-Jan
Easybeats	Friday on my mind	7	04-Jan
Beach Boys	Good vibrations	11	04-Jan
Tom Jones	Green green grass of home	1	04-Jan
Lee Dorsey	Holy cow	14	04-Jan
Elvis Presley	If every day was like Christmas	9	04-Jan
Dave Dee, Dozy, Beaky, Mick & Tich	Save me	3	04-Jan
Donovan	Sunshine superman	2	04-Jan
Roy Orbison	There won't be many coming home	12	04-Jan
Jimmy Ruffin	What becomes of the broken-hearted?	8	04-Jan
Val Doonican	What would I be?	6	04-Jan
Gene Pitney	Just one smile	18	11-Jan
Seekers	Morningtown ride	2	11-Jan
Small Faces	My mind's eye	10	11-Jan
Four Tops	Reach out I'll be there	20	11-Jan
Barron Knights	Under new management	15	11-Jan
Supremes	You keep me hangin' on	8	11-Jan
Temptations	(I know) I'm losing you	19	18-Jan
Troggs	Anyway that you want me	8	18-Jan
Stevie Wonder	A place in the sun	20	25-Jan

Artist	Song	Pos	Date
The Who	Happy Jack	3	25-Jan
Monkees	I'm a believer	1	25-Jan
Cliff Richard & The Shadows	In the country	6	25-Jan
Georgie Fame	Sitting in the park	12	25-Jan
Cream	I feel free	11	01-Feb
The Move	Night of fear	2	01-Feb
Four Tops	Standing in the shadows of love	6	01-Feb
Jimi Hendrix Experience	Hey Joe	6	08-Feb
Cat Stevens	Matthew and son	2	08-Feb
Wayne Fontana	Pamela, Pamela	11	08-Feb
Sandy Posey	Single girl	15	08-Feb
Spencer Davis Group	I'm a man	9	15-Feb
Paul Jones	I've been a bad bad boy	5	15-Feb
Ken Dodd	Let me cry on your shoulder	11	15-Feb
Rolling Stones	Let's spend the night together	3	15-Feb
Nancy Sinatra	Sugar town	8	22-Feb
Petula Clark	This is my song	1	22-Feb
Tremeloes	Here comes my baby	4	01-Mar
Jim Reeves	I won't come in while he's there	12	01-Mar
Marvin Gaye & Kim Weston	It takes two	16	01-Mar
New Vaudeville Band	Peek-a-boo	7	01-Mar
Royal Guardsmen	Snoopy vs The Red Baron	8	01-Mar
Donovan	Mellow yellow	8	08-Mar
Beatles	Penny Lane / Strawberry Fields forever	2	08-Mar
Engelbert Humperdinck	Release me	1	08-Mar
Tom Jones	Detroit City	8	22-Mar
Troggs	Give it to me	12	22-Mar
Herman's Hermits	There's a kind of hush	7	22-Mar
Dusty Springfield	I'll try anything	13	22-Mar

Artist	Song	Pos	Date
Hollies	On a carousel	4	22-Mar
Vince Hill	Edelweiss	2	29-Mar
Seekers	Georgie girl	3	29-Mar
Whistling Jack Smith	I was Kaiser Bill's batman	5	05-Apr
Supremes	Love is here and now you're gone	17	05-Apr
Val Doonican	Memories are made of this	11	05-Apr
Alan Price Set	Simon Smith and the amazing dancing bear	4	05-Apr
Harry Secombe	This is my song	2	05-Apr
Prince Buster	Al Capone	18	12-Apr
Dave Dee, Dozy, Beaky, Mick & Tich	Touch me, touch me	13	12-Apr
Georgie Fame	Because I love you	15	19-Apr
Cliff Richard	It's all over	9	19-Apr
Nancy Sinatra & Frank Sinatra	Somethin' stupid	1	19-Apr
Monkees	A little bit me, a little bit you	3	26-Apr
Pink Floyd	Arnold Layne	20	26-Apr
Four Tops	Bernadette	8	26-Apr
Manfred Mann	Ha! Ha! Said the clown	4	26-Apr
Turtles	Happy together	12	26-Apr
Eddie Floyd	Knock on wood	19	26-Apr
Cat Stevens	I'm gonna get me a gun	6	03-May
Sandie Shaw	Puppet on a string	1	03-May
The Move	I can hear the grass grow	5	10-May
Jimi Hendrix Experience	Purple haze	3	10-May
Jeff Beck	Hi ho silver lining	14	17-May
Lulu	The boat that I row	6	17-May
The Who	Pictures of Lily	4	24-May
Mamas & Papas	Dedicated to the one I love	2	24-May
Tom Jones	Funny familiar forgotten feelings	7	24-May

Artist	Title	Pos	Date
Tremeloes	Silence is golden	1	24-May
Bee Gees	New York mining disaster 1941	12	31-May
Dubliners	Seven drunken nights	7	31-May
Beach Boys	Then I kissed her	4	31-May
Kinks	Waterloo sunset	2	31-May
Jimi Hendrix Experience	The wind cries Mary	6	07-Jun
Procol Harum	A whiter shade of pale	1	14-Jun
New Vaudeville Band	Finchley central	11	14-Jun
Supremes	The happening	6	14-Jun
Vince Hill	Roses of Picardy	13	21-Jun
Arthur Conley	Sweet soul music	7	21-Jun
P.P.Arnold	The first cut is the deepest	18	21-Jun
Engelbert Humperdinck	There goes my everything	2	21-Jun
Hollies	Carrie-Anne	3	28-Jun
Troggs	Night of the long grass	17	28-Jun
Petula Clark	Don't sleep in the subway	12	04-Jul
Young Rascals	Groovin'	8	04-Jul
Dave Dee, Dozy, Beaky, Mick & Tich	Okay!	4	04-Jul
Traffic	Paper sun	5	04-Jul
Small Faces	Here come the nice	12	11-Jul
Turtles	She'd rather be with me	4	11-Jul
Topol	If I were a rich man	9	18-Jul
Aretha Franklin	Respect	10	18-Jul
Cream	Strange brew	17	18-Jul
Beatles	All you need is love	1	25-Jul
Monkees	Alternate title	2	25-Jul
Bachelors	Marta	20	25-Jul
Four Tops	Seven rooms of gloom	12	25-Jul
Marvelettes	When you're young and in love	13	25-Jul
Mike Sammes Singers	Somewhere my love	14	25-Jul

Young Idea	With a little help from my friends	10	25-Jul
Nancy Sinatra / Nancy Sinatra & Lee Hazlewood	You only live twice / Jackson	11	25-Jul
Desmond Dekker & The Aces	007 (Shanty town)	14	01-Aug
Vikki Carr	It must be him	2	01-Aug
Lulu	Let's pretend	11	01-Aug
Pink Floyd	See Emily play	6	01-Aug
Gladys Knight & The Pips	Take me in your arms and love me	13	01-Aug
Dave Davies	Death of a clown	3	08-Aug
Scott McKenzie	San Francisco (Be sure to wear some flowers in your hair)	1	15-Aug
Stevie Wonder	I was made to love her	5	22-Aug
Otis Redding & Carla Thomas	Tramp	18	22-Aug
Johnny Mann Singers	Up, up and away	6	22-Aug
Cat Stevens	A bad night	20	29-Aug
Mamas & Papas	Creeque Alley	9	29-Aug
Tremeloes	Even the bad times are good	4	29-Aug
Amen Corner	Gin house blues	12	29-Aug
Tom Jones	I'll never fall in love again	2	29-Aug
Anita Harris	Just loving you	6	29-Aug
Monkees	Pleasant Valley Sundays	11	29-Aug
Alan Price Set	The house that Jack built	4	05-Sep
Jimi Hendrix Experience	Burning of the midnight lamp	18	12-Sep
Engelbert Humperdinck	The last waltz	1	12-Sep
Rolling Stones	We love you / Dandelion	8	12-Sep
Vanilla Fudge	You keep me hanging on	18	19-Sep

Beach Boys	Heroes and villains	8	19-Sep
Keith West	Excerpt from 'A Teenage Opera'	2	26-Sep
Flower Pot Men	Let's go to San Francisco	4	26-Sep
Small Faces	Itchycoo Park	3	26-Sep
Diana Ross & The Supremes	Reflections	5	03-Oct
Cliff Richard	The day I met Marie	10	03-Oct
The Move	Flowers in the rain	2	10-Oct
Eric Burdon & The Animals	Good times	20	10-Oct
Dubliners	Black velvet band	15	17-Oct
Frankie McBride	Five little fingers	19	17-Oct
Hollies	King Midas in reverse	18	17-Oct
Bee Gees	Massachusetts	1	17-Oct
Frankie Vaughan	There must be a way	7	17-Oct
Traffic	Hole in my shoe	2	24-Oct
Procol Harum	Homburg	6	24-Oct
Box Tops	The letter	5	24-Oct
Seekers	When will the good apples fall	11	24-Oct
Herd	From the underworld	6	07-Nov
Bobbie Gentry	Ode to Billie Joe	13	07-Nov
Dave Dee, Dozy, Beaky, Mick & Tich	Zabadak!	3	07-Nov
Foundations	Baby now that I've found you	1	14-Nov
Sandie Shaw	You've not changed	18	14-Nov
Kinks	Autumn Almanac	3	21-Nov
The Who	I can see for miles	10	21-Nov
Eric Burdon	San Franciscan nights	7	21-Nov
Donovan	There is a mountain	8	21-Nov
Felice Taylor	I feel love coming on	11	28-Nov
Long John Baldry	Let the heartaches begin	1	28-Nov
Troggs	Love is all around	5	28-Nov
Val Doonican	If the whole world stopped loving	3	05-Dec

Dave Clark Five	Everybody knows	2	05-Dec
Des O'Connor	Careless hands	6	12-Dec
Beatles	Hello goodbye	1	12-Dec
Gene Pitney	Something's gotten hold of my heart	5	12-Dec
Bee Gees	World	9	12-Dec
Traffic	Here we go round the Mulberry bush	8	19-Dec
Simon Dupree & The Big Sound	Kites	12	19-Dec
Cliff Richard	All my love	7	26-Dec
Monkees	Daydream believer	8	26-Dec
Tom Jones	I'm coming home	2	26-Dec
Diana Ross & The Supremes	In and out of love	17	26-Dec
Beatles	Magical Mystery Tour - EP (Magical mystery tour / Your mother should know / I am the walrus)	3	26-Dec
Scaffold	Thank u very much	9	26-Dec
Small Faces	Tin soldier	18	26-Dec
Four Tops	Walk away Renee	16	26-Dec

The events ....

- Milton Keynes, a village in North Buckinghamshire, was formally designated as a new town by the government[104],[105],[106]
- The British-designed satellite Ariel 3, the first to be developed outside the Soviet Union or United States was launched[107]
- The Roman Catholic Liverpool Metropolitan Cathedral of Christ the King was consecrated[110]
- Dunsop Valley entered the UK Weather Records with the highest 90-minute total rainfall at 117 mm[110]
- A Court in Brighton was the first in England and Wales to decide a case by majority verdict (10 to 2) of the jury[120]
- Charles de Gaulle vetoed British entry into the European Economic Community again[108]

Liverpool Metropolitan Cathedral
© David Iliff (2014) / Wikimedia Commons / CC BY-SA

- St Christopher's Hospice, the world's first purpose-built secular hospice specialising in the palliative care of the terminally ill, was established in South London by Cicely Saunders[109]

In the world of sport ......

- England's World Cup winning manager Alf Ramsey received a knighthood and Captain Bobby Moore an OBE in the New Year's Honours[110]

Alf Ramsey
© *Bert Verhoeff (1969) /*
Wikimedia Commons /
CC BY-SA 3.0
Netherlands

Bobby Moore
Credit: National Media Museum (1966) /
Wikimedia Commons / Public Domain

- Queens Park Rangers became the first Football League 3rd division side to win the League Cup at Wembley Stadium defeating West Bromwich Albion 3-2[110]
- Manchester United won the Football League First Division title[111]
- In the first all-London FA Cup Final, Tottenham Hotspur defeated Chelsea 2-1 at Wembley Stadium[112]
- Boxer Henry Cooper became the first to win three Lonsdale Belts outright[120]
- Celtic F.C. became the first British and Northern European team to reach a European Cup Final and win it, beating Inter Milan 2-1 in Lisbon, Portugal[110]
- Sir Francis Chichester arrived in Plymouth after completing his single-handed sailing voyage around the world in his yacht, Gipsy Moth IV, in nine months and one day[113]
- In the last amateur Wimbledon tennis tournament, the Gentlemen's Singles title was won by Australian Jon Newcombe and the Ladies' Singles title was won by American Billie Jean King[110]

Henry Cooper
Credit: Wikimedia Commons (1969) /
Public Domain

In the world of entertainment.......

- The Beatles released the album *'Sgt.Pepper's Lonely Hearts Club Band'*[110]
- The first scheduled colour television broadcast began on BBC2 with the first live coverage of the Wimbledon Championships[114]
- Pink Floyd released their debut album *'The Piper at the Gates of Dawn'*[110]
- The UK Marine Broadcasting Offences Act declared participation in offshore pirate radio illegal and consequently Radio London and Radio Scotland shut down. Radio Caroline however, continued to broadcast illegally from vessels off the Isle of Man and off the Essex coast[110]
- Prime Minister Harold Wilson won a libel action against rock group The Move after they depicted him in the nude in promotional material for their record 'Flowers in the Rain'[115]
- Rolling Stones guitarist Brian Jones won a High Court appeal against a 9 month prison sentence for possessing and using Cannabis, and was instead fined £1000 and put on probation for three years[116]
- BBC Radio 4 panel game *'Just a Minute'*, chaired by Nicholas Parsons, was first transmitted and would still be running more than 40 years later[110]
- The Bee Gees signed a management contract with Robert Stigwood[117]
- The musical film *Cuckoo Patrol* was released starring Freddie Garrity[117]
- The Daily Mail reported on 4,000 potholes in Blackburn, Lancs and the death of the Guinness heiress Tara Brown, which inspired the lyrics for The Beatles song *'A Day in the Life'*[117]
- Micky Dolenz of the Monkees watched the programme *'Till Death Us Do Part'* on British TV and used the term *'Randy Scouse Git'* from the program for the title of the Monkees next single release, not realising it to be an offensive term. British censors forced the title to be changed to *'Alternate Title'* in the UK[117]
- John Lennon and Paul McCartney were awarded the Ivor Novello award for "Michelle"[117]
- The 12th Eurovision Song Contest was held in Vienna, Austria and was won by the UK for the first time with the song *'Puppet On A String'* sung by Sandie Shaw[110]

The Move
Credit: Deram / London Records (1967) / Wikimedia Commons / Public Domain

The Monkees
Credit: NBC Television (1966) / Wikimedia Commons / Public Domain

Freddie Garrity
Credit: KRLA Beat (1965) / Wikimedia Commons / Public Domain

- Pink Floyd staged the first ever rock concert with quadrophonic sound at Queen Elizabeth Hall, London[117]
- The Beatles performed *'All You Need Is Love'* for the *'Our World'* television special, the first worldwide television broadcast. Backing singers included Eric Clapton and members of the Rolling Stones and The Who[117]
- Mick Jagger and Keith Richard were sentenced to jail for drug possession and later appealed successfully against their sentences[110]
- The musical film *Doctor Doolittle* was released starring Rex Harrison, Samantha Eggar and Anthony Newley[117]
- The musical film *Half a Sixpence* was released starring Tommy Steele[117]
- The musical film *The Mini-Affair* was released starring Georgie Fame[117]
- The musical film *Privilege* was released starring Paul Jones[117]
- BBC Radio 1 was launched by Tony Blackburn playing *'Flowers in the Rain'* by The Move[118]
- John Entwistle of The Who married former school friend Alison Wise[119]

Georgie Fame
Credit: Pressens Bild (1968) / Wikimedia Commons / Public Domain

Paul Jones
© Eric Koch / Anefo (1967) / Wikimedia Commons / CC BY-SA 3.0 Unported

In the world of business.....

- The first automatic voucher-based cash machine was installed at the office of Barclay's Bank in Enfield[120]
- The first stage of Cumbernauld town centre, the main shopping centre of the New Town of Cumbernauld, Scotland, was completed and widely accepted as the UK's first shopping mall and the world's first multi-level covered town centre[121]
- Car manufacturer Chrysler took full control of the Rootes Group[122]
- The Beatles opened the Apple boutique in London[110]

In the world of education.....

- Tony O'Connor became the first black headmaster of a British school, in Warley, near Birmingham, Worcestershire[110]

In the world of transport.....

- Ford announced the end of the Anglia production and replaced it with an all-new car called the Escort[110]
- The Concorde supersonic aircraft was unveiled in Toulouse, France[110]
- The RMS *Queen Elizabeth 2* was launched at Clydebank by Queen Elizabeth II, using the same pair of gold scissors used by her mother and grandmother to launch the *Queen Elizabeth* and *Queen Mary* respectively[123]

Concorde
© *Eduard Marmet (1986) / Wikimedia Commons / CC BY-SA 3.0 Unported*

RMS Queen Elizabeth II
Credit: Tim Dyer (2007) / Wikimedia Commons / Public Domain

1968

Welcome to the lighter side of life in Britain in 1968

The music ……

Artist	Title	Highest position this year	W/E date
Cliff Richard	All my love	6	02-Jan
Des O'Connor	Careless hands	11	02-Jan
Dave Clark Five	Everybody knows	16	02-Jan
Beatles	Hello goodbye	1	02-Jan
Val Doonican	If the whole world stopped loving	4	02-Jan
Tom Jones	I'm coming home	3	02-Jan
Long John Baldry	Let the heartches begin	8	02-Jan
Beatles	Magical Mystery Tour - EP (Magical mystery tour / Your mother should know / I am the walrus)	2	02-Jan
Gene Pitney	Something's gotten hold of my heart	5	02-Jan
Englebert Humperdinck	The last waltz	13	02-Jan
Frankie Vaughan	There must be a way	20	02-Jan
Diana Ross & The Supremes	In and out of love	13	09-Jan
Simon Dupree & The Big Sound	Kites	9	09-Jan
Dave Davies	Susannah's still alive	20	09-Jan
Scaffold	Thank u very much	4	09-Jan
Monkees	Daydream believer	5	16-Jan
Traffic	Here we go round the Mulberry Bush	10	16-Jan
Petula Clark	The other man's grass (is always greener)	20	16-Jan

73

Artist	Song	#	Date
Four Tops	Walk away Renee	3	16-Jan
Bee Gees	World	11	23-Jan
Englebert Humperdinck	Am I that easy to forget?	3	30-Jan
Herd	Paradise lost	15	30-Jan
Georgie Fame	The ballad of Bonnie and Clyde	1	30-Jan
Small Faces	Tin soldier	9	30-Jan
Love Affair	Everlasting love	1	06-Feb
Plastic Penny	Everything I am	6	06-Feb
Alan Price Set	Don't stop the carnival	13	13-Feb
Brenton Wood	Gimme little sign	8	13-Feb
Herman's Hermits	I can take or leave your loving	11	13-Feb
John Fred & The Playboy Band	Judy in disguise (with glasses)	3	13-Feb
Tremeloes	Suddenly you love me	6	13-Feb
Foundations	Back on my feet again	18	20-Feb
Amen Corner	Bend me, shape me	3	20-Feb
Moody Blues	Nights in white satin	19	20-Feb
Manfred Mann	The Mighty Quinn	1	20-Feb
Status Quo	Pictures of matchstick men	7	27-Feb
Solomon King	She wears my ring	3	27-Feb
Esther & Abi Ofarim	Cinderella Rockefella	1	05-Mar
Bee Gees	Words	8	05-Mar
Beach Boys	Darlin'	11	19-Mar
The Move	Fire Brigade	3	19-Mar
Lemon Pipers	Green tambourine	7	19-Mar
Donovan	Jennifer Juniper	5	19-Mar
Don Partridge	Rosie	4	19-Mar
Lulu	Me, the peaceful heart	9	26-Mar
Dave Dee, Dozy, Beaky, Mick & Tich	The legend of Xanadu	1	26-Mar
Otis Redding	(Sittin' on) The dock of the bay	3	02-Apr
Tom Jones	Delilah	2	02-Apr
Elvis Presley	Guitar man	19	02-Apr

Artist	Title	Weeks	Date
Beatles	Lady Madonna	1	02-Apr
Four Tops	If I were a carpenter	7	09-Apr
Paul Mauriat	Love is blue (L'amour est bleu)	12	09-Apr
Reparata & The Delrons	Captain of your ship	13	16-Apr
Cliff Richard	Congratulations	1	16-Apr
Bill Haley & His Comets	Rock around the clock	20	16-Apr
Cilla Black	Step inside love	8	16-Apr
Monkees	Valleri	12	16-Apr
John Rowles	If I only had time	3	23-Apr
Hollies	Jennifer Eccles	7	23-Apr
Showstoppers	Ain't nothin' but a house party	11	30-Apr
Box Tops	Cry like a baby	15	30-Apr
Easybeats	Hello, how are you?	20	30-Apr
Honeybus	I can't let Maggie go	8	30-Apr
Louis Armstrong	What a wonderful world / Cabaret	1	30-Apr
Andy Williams	Can't take my eyes off you	5	07-May
1910 Fruitgum Company	Simon says	2	07-May
Paper Dolls	Something here in my heart	11	07-May
Gene Pitney	Somewhere in the country	19	07-May
Herd	I don't want our loving to die	5	14-May
Small Faces	Lazy Sunday	2	14-May
Roger Miller	Little green apples	19	14-May
Jackie	White horses	10	21-May
Englebert Humperdinck	A man without love	2	21-May
Tremeloes	Helule Helule	14	28-May
Herman's Hermits	Sleepy Joe	12	28-May
Gary Puckett & The Union Gap	Young girl	1	28-May
Bobby Goldsboro	Honey	2	04-Jun
Dionne Warwick	Do you know the way to San Jose?	8	11-Jun

Scott Walker	Joanna	7	11-Jun
Love Affair	Rainbow valley	5	11-Jun
Elvis Presley	U.S.Male	15	11-Jun
Don Partridge	Blue eyes	3	25-Jun
Donovan	Hurdy Gurdy Man	4	25-Jun
Rolling Stones	Jumping Jack Flash	1	25-Jun
Julie Driscoll, Brian Auger & The Trinity	This wheel's on fire	5	25-Jun
Lulu	Boy	15	02-Jul
Equals	Baby come back	1	09-Jul
John Rowles	Hush…not a word to Mary	12	09-Jul
Marmalade	Lovin' things	6	09-Jul
O.C.Smith	The son of Hickory Holler's tramp	2	09-Jul
Monkees	D.W.Washburn	17	16-Jul
Manfred Mann	My name is Jack	8	16-Jul
Cupid's Inspiration	Yesterday has gone	4	16-Jul
Esther & Abi Ofarim	One more dance	13	23-Jul
Ohio Express	Yummy yummy yummy	5	23-Jul
Des O'Connor	I pretend	1	30-Jul
Richard Harris	MacArthur Park	4	30-Jul
Sue Nicholls	Where will you be?	17	30-Jul
R.Dean Taylor	Gotta see Jane	17	06-Aug
Dave Dee, Dozy, Beaky, Mick & Tich	Last night in Soho	8	06-Aug
Tommy James & The Shondells	Mony Mony	1	06-Aug
Small Faces	Universal	16	06-Aug
Simon & Garfunkel	Mrs.Robinson	4	13-Aug
Pigmeat Markham	Here comes the judge	19	13-Aug
Sly & The Family Stone	Dance to the music	7	20-Aug
Kinks	Days	12	20-Aug
Crazy World Of Arthur Brown	Fire!	1	20-Aug
Dusty Springfield	I close my eyes and count to ten	4	20-Aug
Herb Alpert	This guy's in love with you	3	20-Aug

Artist	Song		Date
Herman's Hermits	Sunshine girl	8	20-Aug
Tom Jones	Help yourself	5	27-Aug
Beach Boys	Do it again	1	03-Sep
Bruce Chanel	Keep on	12	03-Sep
Amen Corner	High in the sky	6	10-Sep
Aretha Franklin	I say a little prayer	4	10-Sep
Bee Gees	I've gotta get a message to you	1	10-Sep
Mama Cass	Dream a little dream of me	11	17-Sep
Beatles	Hey Jude	1	17-Sep
Johnny Nash	Hold me tight	5	17-Sep
Otis Redding	Hard to handle	15	24-Sep
Canned Heat	On the road again	8	24-Sep
Vanity Fare	I live for the sun	20	01-Oct
Mary Hopkin	Those were the days	1	01-Oct
Mason Williams	Classical gas	9	15-Oct
Doors	Hello I love you	15	15-Oct
Status Quo	Ice in the sun	8	15-Oct
Gary Puckett & The Union Gap	Lady Willpower	5	15-Oct
Leapy Lee	Little arrows	2	15-Oct
Tremeloes	My little lady	6	15-Oct
Dave Clark Five	The red balloon	7	15-Oct
Casuals	Jesamine	2	22-Oct
Love Affair	A day without love	6	29-Oct
Englebert Humperdinck	Les bicyclettes de Belsize	5	29-Oct
Hollies	Listen to me	11	29-Oct
Jose Feliciano	Light my fire	6	05-Nov
Marbles	Only one woman	5	05-Nov
Dave Dee, Dozy, Beaky, Mick & Tich	The wreck of the Antoinette	14	05-Nov
Joe Cocker	With a little help from my friends	1	12-Nov
Hugo Montenegro	The good, the bad, and the ugly	1	19-Nov
Marvin Gaye & Tammi Terrell	You're all I need to get by	19	19-Nov
Johnny Johnson & His Bandwagon	Breakin' down the walls of heartache	4	26-Nov

Turtles	Elenore	7	26-Nov
Barry Ryan	Elouise	2	26-Nov
Val Doonican	If I knew then what I know now	14	26-Nov
Long John Baldry	Mexico	15	26-Nov
Isley Brothers	This old heart of mine	3	26-Nov
Jimi Hendrix Experience	All along the watchtower	5	03-Dec
Lulu	I'm a tiger	9	03-Dec
Jeannie C.Riley	Harper Valley P.T.A.	12	10-Dec
Malcolm Roberts	May I have the next dream with you?	8	10-Dec
Des O'Connor	1-2-3 O'Leary	4	17-Dec
Scaffold	Lily the pink	1	17-Dec
Diana Ross & The Supremes	Love child	17	17-Dec
Nina Simone	Ain't got no - I got life / Do what you gotta do	2	24-Dec
Bonzo Dog Doo-Dah Band	I'm the urban spaceman	5	24-Dec
Judy Clay & William Bell	Private number	14	24-Dec
Gun	Race with the devil	8	24-Dec
Dusty Springfield	Son of a preacher man	20	24-Dec
Tom Jones	A minute of your time	14	31-Dec
Fleetwood Mac	Albatross	9	31-Dec
Foundations	Build me up buttercup	2	31-Dec
Marmalade	Ob-la-di, ob-la-da	7	31-Dec
Love Scultpture	Sabre dance	5	31-Dec

The events ……..

- Northampton, the county town of Northamptonshire, was designated as a New Town with the government hoping to double its population by 1980[124]
- Coal mining in the Black Country, which played a big part in the Industrial Revolution, ended after some 300 years with the closure of Baggeridge Colliery near Sedgeley[125]

- Mr Frederick West became Britain's first heart transplant patient[126]
- The General Post Office divided the post into first-class and second-class services[127]
- The Dawley New Town (Designation) Amendment (Telford) Order extended the boundaries of Dawley New Town in Shropshire and renamed it Telford[141]

In the world of sport ……

- Great Britain and Northern Ireland competed at the Winter Olympics in Grenoble, France, but did not win any medals[141]
- Manchester City won the Football League First Division title[128]
- West Bromwich Albion won the FA Cup for the fifth time, with Jeff Astle scoring the only goal of the game against Everton at Wembley Stadium[141]
- Manchester United became the first English winners of the European Cup after beating Benfica 4-1 in extra-time at Wembley Stadium[129]
- Alec Rose returned from a 354-day single-handed round-the-world trip for which he received a knighthood the following day[130]
- Great Britain and Northern Ireland competed at the Summer Olympics in Mexico City and won 5 gold, 5 silver and 3 bronze medals[141]

In the world of entertainment…….

- The first performance of an Andrew Lloyd-Webber / Tim Rice musical, *'Joseph and the Amazing Technicolor Dreamcoat'* in its original form as a 'pop cantata' was given by pupils of Colet Court preparatory school in Hammersmith[131],[132],[133]
- The Beatles animated film, *'Yellow Submarine'*, debuted in London[139]
- The BBC sitcom *'Dad's Army'* was first aired on television[141]
- The first Isle of Wight festival took place[141]
- The U.S. musical *'Hair'* opened in London following the removal of theatre censorship[134]

The Kinks
Credit: Wikimedia Commons
(1965) / Public Domain

- *'The Kinks Are The Village Green Preservation Society'* was released[135]
- Arthur C. Clarke's novel *'2001: A Space Odyssey'* was published[141]
- The 13th Eurovision Song Contest was held in London with United Kingdom's entry, *"Congratulations"* sung by Cliff Richard, finishing second behind the entry from Spain[136]
- The Beatles *'White Album'* was released[136]
- Trojan Records was founded by Lee Gopthal[136]
- Bill Medley left The Righteous Brothers to pursue a solo career[137]

- Sandie Shaw secretly married fashion designer Jeff Banks at Greenwich Registry Office in London[138]

In the world of business.....

- London Bridge was sold to American entrepreneur Robert P. McCulloch and was rebuilt at Lake Havasu City, Arizona[139]

London Bridge, Lake Havasu, Arizona
© Ken Lund (2009) / Wikimedia Commons / CC BY-SA 2.0 Generic

In the world of transport.....

- The M1 motorway was completed by the opening of the final 35-mile section between Rotherham and Leeds[140]
- The Ford Escort was introduced to replace the Anglia[141]

Ford Escort Mk 1
© Charles01 (2010) / Wikimedia Commons / CC BY-SA 3.0 Unported

1969

Welcome to the lighter side of life in Britain in 1969

The music ……

Artist	Title	Highest position this year	W/E date
Des O'Connor	1-2-3 O'Leary	8	07-Jan
Tom Jones	A minute of your time	17	07-Jan
Nina Simone	Ain't got no - I got life / Do what you gotta do	7	07-Jan
Johnny Johnson & His Bandwagon	Breakin' down the walls of heartache	19	07-Jan
Bonzo Dog Doo-Dah Band	I'm the urban spaceman	5	07-Jan
Malcolm Roberts	May I have the next dream with you?	16	07-Jan
Marmalade	Ob-la-di, ob-la-da	1	07-Jan
Bedrocks	Ob-la-di, ob-la-da	20	07-Jan
Gun	Race with the devil	11	07-Jan
Love Scultpture	Sabre dance	6	07-Jan
Dusty Springfield	Son of a preacher man	9	07-Jan
Hugo Montenegro	The good, the bad, and the ugly	15	07-Jan
Foundations	Build me up buttercup	2	14-Jan
Lulu	I'm a tiger	11	14-Jan
Scaffold	Lily the pink	1	14-Jan
Diana Ross & The Supremes	Love child	15	14-Jan
Isley Brothers	This old heart of mine	20	14-Jan
Herman's Hermits	Something's happening	6	21-Jan
Stevie Wonder	For once in my life	3	28-Jan

Artist	Title	Pos	Date
Judy Clay & William Bell	Private number	8	28-Jan
Fleetwood Mac	Albatross	1	04-Feb
Manfred Mann	Fox on the run	5	04-Feb
Kasenetz-Katz Singing Orchestral Circus	Quick Joey Small (run Joey run)	19	04-Feb
Edwin Starr	Stop her on sight / Headline news	11	04-Feb
The Move	Blackberry Way	1	11-Feb
Martha Reeves & The Vandellas	Dancing in the street	4	11-Feb
Simon & Garfunkel	Mrs.Robinson - EP (Mrs Robinson / April come she will)	9	11-Feb
Tymes	People	16	11-Feb
Nina Simone	To love somebody	5	11-Feb
Johnny Nash	You got soul	6	11-Feb
Canned Heat	Going up the country	19	18-Feb
Amen Corner	(If paradise is) Half as nice	1	18-Feb
Wilson Pickett	Hey Jude	16	18-Feb
Isley Brothers	I guess I'll always love you	11	18-Feb
Diana Ross & The Supremes & The Temptations	I'm gonna make you love me	3	25-Feb
Marv Johnson	I'll pick a rose for my rose	10	04-Mar
Peter Sarstedt	Where do you go to (my lovely)	1	04-Mar
Donald Peers	Please don't go	3	11-Mar
Sam & Dave	Soul sister, brown sugar	15	11-Mar
Glen Campbell	Wichita lineman	7	11-Mar
Bee Gees	First of May	6	18-Mar
Engelbert Humperdinck	The way it used to be	3	18-Mar
Elvis Presley	If I can dream	11	25-Mar
Love Affair	One road	16	25-Mar
Righteous Brothers	You've lost that lovin' feeling'	10	25-Mar

Artist	Song	Weeks	Date
Joe South	Games people play	6	01-Apr
Temptations	Get ready	10	01-Apr
Cliff Richard	Good times	12	01-Apr
Marvin Gaye	I heard it through the grapevine	1	01-Apr
Cilla Black	Surround yourself with sorrow	3	01-Apr
Dean Martin	Gentle on my mind	2	08-Apr
Sandie Shaw	Monsieur Dupont	6	08-Apr
Hollies	Sorry Suzanne	3	08-Apr
Lulu	Boom bang-a-bang	2	15-Apr
Beach Boys	I can hear music	10	15-Apr
Foundations	In the bad, bad old days	8	15-Apr
Mary Hopkin	Goodbye	2	22-Apr
Tremeloes	Hello world	14	22-Apr
Desmond Dekker & The Aces	The Israelites	1	22-Apr
Beatles & Billy Preston	Get back	1	29-Apr
Stevie Wonder	I don't know why I love you	14	29-Apr
The Who	Pinball wizard	4	29-Apr
Johnny Nash	Cupid	6	06-May
Bob & Earl	Harlem shuffle	7	06-May
Noel Harrison	The windmills of your mind	8	06-May
Cream	Badge	18	13-May
Clodagh Rodgers	Come back and shake me	3	13-May
Diana Ross & The Supremes	I'm living in shame	14	13-May
Sarah Vaughan & Billy Eckstine	Passing strangers	20	13-May
Jr. Walker & The Allstars	Road runner	12	13-May
Herman's Hermits	My sentimental friend	2	20-May
Isley Brothers	Behind a painted smile	5	27-May
5th Dimension	Aquarius / Let the sun shine in	11	03-Jun

Artist	Title		
Des O'Connor	Dick-a-dum-dum (King's Road)	14	03-Jun
Tom Jones	Love me tonight	9	03-Jun
Fleetwood Mac	Man of the world	2	03-Jun
Frank Sinatra	My way	5	03-Jun
Manfred Mann	Ragamuffin man	8	03-Jun
Tommy Roe	Dizzy	1	10-Jun
Glen Campbell	Galveston	14	10-Jun
Simon & Garfunkel	The boxer	6	10-Jun
Jackie Wilson	(Your love keeps lifting me) Higher and higher	11	17-Jun
Beatles	The ballad of John and Yoko	1	17-Jun
Smokey Robinson & The Miracles	The tracks of my tears	9	17-Jun
Cliff Richard	Big ship	8	24-Jun
Chicken Shack	I'd rather go blind	14	24-Jun
Edwin Hawkins Singers	Oh happy day	2	24-Jun
Booker T & The MG's	Time is tight	4	24-Jun
Andy Williams	Happy heart	19	01-Jul
Jethro Tull	Living in the past	3	01-Jul
Four Tops	What is a man?	16	01-Jul
Peter Sarstedt	Frozen orange juice	10	08-Jul
Crazy Elephant	Gimme, gimme, good loving	12	08-Jul
Elvis Presley	In the ghetto	2	08-Jul
Thunderclap Newman	Something in the air	1	08-Jul
Beach Boys	Breakaway	6	15-Jul
Amen Corner	Hello Suzie	4	15-Jul
Scott Walker	Lights of Cincinnati	13	15-Jul
Creedence Clearwater Revival	Proud Mary	8	15-Jul
Marmalade	Baby make it soon	9	22-Jul
Desmond Dekker & The Aces	It miek	7	22-Jul
Family Dogg	Way of life	6	22-Jul
John Lennon & Yoko One With The Plastic Ono Band	Give peace a chance	2	29-Jul

Artist	Title		Date
Rolling Stones	Honky Tonk women	1	29-Jul
Donovan & Jeff Beck Group	Goo Goo Barabajagal (Love is hot)	12	02-Aug
Billy Preston	That's the way God planned it	11	02-Aug
Clodagh Rodgers	Goodnight midnight	4	09-Aug
Dells	I can sing a rainbow - love is blue (medley)	15	09-Aug
Georgie Fame	Peaceful	16	09-Aug
Love Affair	Bringing on back the good times	9	16-Aug
Cilla Black	Conversations	7	16-Aug
Vanity Fare	Early in the morning	8	16-Aug
Joe Dolan	Make me an island	3	16-Aug
Robin Gibb	Saved by the bell	2	16-Aug
Max Romeo	Wet dream	10	16-Aug
Jim Reeves	When two worlds collide	17	16-Aug
The Move	Curly	12	23-Aug
Stevie Wonder	My cherie amour	4	23-Aug
Zager & Evans	In the year 2525 (Exordium and Terminus)	1	30-Aug
Equals	Viva Bobby Joe	6	30-Aug
Engelbert Humperdinck	I'm a better man	15	13-Sep
Crosby, Still & Nash	Marrakesh Express	17	13-Sep
Humble Pie	Natural born boogie	4	13-Sep
Marvin Gaye	Too busy thinking 'bout my baby	5	13-Sep
Creedence Clearwater Revival	Bad moon rising	1	20-Sep
Peddlers	Birth	17	20-Sep
Bee Gees	Don't forget to remember	2	20-Sep
Temptations	Cloud nine	15	27-Sep
Isley Brothers	Put yourself in my place	13	27-Sep
Johnny Cash	A boy named Sue	4	04-Oct
Oliver	Good morning starshine	6	04-Oct
Mama Cass	It's getting better	8	04-Oct

Artist	Song	Weeks	Date
Radha Krishna Temple	Hare Krishna mantra	12	04-Oct
Diana Ross & The Supremes & The Temptations	I second that emotion	18	04-Oct
Cliff Richard	Throw down a line	7	04-Oct
Jane Birkin & Serge Gainsbourg	Je t'aime….moi non plus	1	11-Oct
Bob Dylan	Lay lady lay	5	11-Oct
Bobbie Gentry	I'll never fall in love again	1	18-Oct
Sounds Nice feat. Tim Mycroft	Love at first sight (Je t'aime….moi non plus)	18	18-Oct
Karen Young	Nobody's child	6	18-Oct
Four Tops	Do what you gotta do	11	25-Oct
Archies	Sugar sugar	1	25-Oct
Hollies	He ain't heavy…he's my brother	3	01-Nov
Lou Christie	I'm gonna make you mine	2	01-Nov
David Bowie	Space oddity	5	01-Nov
Joe Cocker	Delta lady	10	08-Nov
Frank Sinatra	Love's been good to me	8	08-Nov
Fleetwood Mac	Oh well	2	08-Nov
Upsetters	Return of Django / Dollar in the teeth	5	08-Nov
Jr.Walker & The Allstars	What does it take (to win your love)?	13	15-Nov
John Lennon & Yoko One With The Plastic Ono Band	Cold turkey	14	15-Nov
Tremeloes	(Call me) Number one	2	22-Nov
Beatles	Something / Come together	4	22-Nov
Jethro Tull	Sweet dream	7	22-Nov
Joe Dolan	Teresa	20	22-Nov
Jimmy Cliff	Wonderful world, beautiful people	6	22-Nov

Harry J. & The All Stars	The Liquidator	9	29-Nov
Stevie Wonder	Yester-me, yester-you, yesterday	2	06-Dec
Malcolm Roberts	Love is all	12	13-Dec
Blue Mink	Melting pot	5	13-Dec
Kenny Rogers & The First Edition	Ruby, don't take your love to town	2	13-Dec
Marvin Gaye & Tammi Terrell	The onion song	9	13-Dec
Engelbert Humperdinck	Winter world of love	7	13-Dec
Bobbie Gentry & Glen Campbell	All I have to do is dream	7	20-Dec
Rolf Harris	Two little boys	1	20-Dec
Cliff Richard	With the eyes of a child	20	20-Dec
Jim Reeves	But you love me Daddy	17	27-Dec
Roger Whittaker	Durham Town (the leavin')	13	27-Dec
Dave Clark Five	Good old rock 'n' roll	12	27-Dec
Creedence Clearwater Revival	Green river	19	27-Dec
Des O'Connor	Loneliness	18	27-Dec
Elvis Presley	Suspicious minds	4	27-Dec
Cufflinks	Tracy	9	27-Dec
Tom Jones	Without love	10	27-Dec

The events ....

- The Space Hopper toy was first introduced[142]
- Swansea was granted city status[149]
- Golden eagles were found to be nesting in England for the first time in modern history, at Haweswater in the Lake District[143]

In the world of sport ......

- Sir Matt Busby, hugely successful manager of Manchester United F.C. for 24 years, announced his retirement at the end of the season[144]

Golden eagle
© *Tony Hisgett (2011) /*
Wikimedia Commons /
CC BY 2.0 Generic

- Robin Knox-Johnston became the first person to sail around the world solo without stopping[149]
- Manchester City F.C. beat Leicester City 1-0 to win the FA Cup at Wembley Stadium[145]
- Leeds United won the Football League First Division title for the first time in their history[146]
- Golfer Tony Jacklin won the Open Championship[147]

In the world of entertainment……..

- The Beatles gave their last public performance, on the roof of Apple Records. The impromptu concert was broken up by the Police[147]
- Pop singer Lulu married Maurice Gibb of the Bee Gees[148]

Lulu
© Wikimedia Commons (2010) / CC BY-SA 3.0

Maurice Gibb
© AVRO (1973) / Wikimedia Commons / CC BY-SA 3.0 Unported

Paul & Linda McCartney
© Jim Summaria (1976) / Wikimedia Commons / CC BY-SA 3.0 Unported

- Paul McCartney married Linda Eastman[147]
- John Lennon and Yoko Ono married in Gibraltar[149]
- The UK shared first place in the Eurovision Song Contest with the entry *Boom bang-a-bang* sung by Lulu[149]
- The final episode of the long-running BBC Radio serial drama 'Mrs Dale's Diary' was broadcast[147]
- The Who released their concept album '*Tommy*'[149]
- The showing of the television documentary 'The Royal Family' attracted more than 30.6 million viewers, an all-time British record for a non-current event programme[150],[151]

John Lennon & Yoko Ono
© Jack Mitchell / Wikimedia Commons / CC BY-SA 4.0 International

- The second Isle of Wight festival attracted 150,000 people with the appearance of Bob Dylan being a major incentive[152]
- The Beatles released their final album '*Abbey Road*'[149]
- '*Monty Python's Flying Circus*' was first aired on the BBC[147]
- Regular colour television broadcasts began on BBC1 and ITV[153]

- The 6th James Bond film – '*On Her Majesty's Secret Service*' – was released with George Lazenby taking the lead[154]
- Fairport Convention released their pioneering folk rock album *Liege & Lief*[155]
- James Galway began a 6-year engagement as principal flautist with the Berlin Philharmonic Orchestra[155]
- The musical film *Can Heironymus Merkin Ever Forget Mercy Humppe and Find True Happiness?* starring Anthony Newley was released[155]
- Kiki Dee became the first British girl singer to be signed by the Motown record label in Detroit[156]

Kiki Dee
Credit: MCA Records (1974) / Wikimedia Commons / Public Domain

In the world of business…..

- The British Sunday newspaper *The News of the World* was purchased by Australian media baron Rupert Murdoch[157]
- The first B&Q DIY superstore was established in Southampton by Richard Block and David Quayle[158],[159]
- The pre-decimal halfpenny piece ceased to be legal tender[147]
- The new seven-sided 50p coin was introduced as the replacement for the 10-shilling note[160]
- '*The Sun*' newspaper was re-launched as a tabloid under the ownership of Rupert Murdoch[149]

Ford Capri Mk 1
© Charles01 (2009) / Wikimedia Commons / CC BY-SA 3.0 Unported

In the world of transport…..

- Ford launched the Capri, a four-seater sporting coupe designed to compete with the likes of the MG B[161]
- The London Underground Victoria line was opened by The Queen[147]
- British Leyland Motor Company launched Britain's first production hatch back car, the Austin Maxi, designed to compete with family saloons such as the Ford Cortina[162]
- The maiden flight of Concorde took place[147]

Austin Maxi Mk 1 (left) & Mk 2 (right)
© Lanmax69 (2013) / Wikimedia Commons / CC BY-SA 3.0 Unported

Alphabetical listing by artist

Artist	Title	Year
1910 Fruitgum Company	Simon says	1968
5th Dimension	Aquarius / Let the sun shine in	1969
Adam Faith	A message to Martha (Kentucky Bluebird)	1964 1965
Adam Faith	As you like it	1962
Adam Faith	Don't that beat all	1962
Adam Faith	Don't you know it ?	1961
Adam Faith	Easy going me	1961
Adam Faith	How about that !	1960
Adam Faith	Lonely pup (in a Christmas shop)	1960 1961
Adam Faith	Lonesome	1962
Adam Faith	Made you	1960
Adam Faith	Poor me	1960
Adam Faith	Someone else's baby	1960
Adam Faith	The first time	1963
Adam Faith	The time has come	1961
Adam Faith	This is it	1961
Adam Faith	We are in love	1964
Adam Faith	What do you want?	1960
Adam Faith	When Johnny comes marching home	1960
Adam Faith	Who am I	1961
Alan Price Set	Don't stop the carnival	1968
Alan Price Set	Hi-lili, hi-lo	1966
Alan Price Set	I put a spell on you	1966
Alan Price Set	Simon Smith and the amazing dancing bear	1967
Alan Price Set	The house that Jack built	1967
Allan Sherman	Hello Muddah! Hello Fadduh!	1963
Allisons	Are you sure ?	1961
Amen Corner	(If paradise is) half as nice	1969
Amen Corner	Bend me, shape me	1968
Amen Corner	Gin house blues	1967
Amen Corner	Hello Suzie	1969
Amen Corner	High in the sky	1968

Andy Stewart	A Scottish soldier (green hills of Tyrol)	1961
Andy Williams	Almost there	1965
Andy Williams	Can't get used to losing you	1963
Andy Williams	Can't take my eyes off you	1968
Andy Williams	Happy heart	1969
Andy Williams	May each day	1966
Animals	Bring it on home to me	1965
Animals	Don't bring me down	1966
Animals	Don't let me be misunderstood	1965
Animals	House of the rising sun	1964
Animals	I'm crying	1964
Animals	Inside - looking out	1966
Animals	It's my life	1965
Animals	We gotta get out of this place	1965
Anita Harris	Just loving you	1967
Anne Shelton	Sailor	1961
Anthony Newley	And the heaven's cried	1961
Anthony Newley	Bee bom	1961
Anthony Newley	Do you mind?	1960
Anthony Newley	If she should come to you	1960
Anthony Newley	Pop goes the weasel	1961
Anthony Newley	Strawberry fair	1960 1961
Anthony Newley	Why	1960
Applejacks	Like dreamers do	1964
Applejacks	Tell me when	1964
Archies	Sugar sugar	1969
Aretha Franklin	I say a little prayer	1968
Aretha Franklin	Respect	1967
Arthur Conley	Sweet soul music	1967
Avons	Seven little girls (sitting in the back seat)	1960
B.Bumble & The Stingers	Nut rocker	1962
Bachelors	Charmaine	1963
Bachelors	Diane	1964
Bachelors	I believe	1964
Bachelors	I wouldn't trade you for the world	1964
Bachelors	Marie	1965
Bachelors	Marta	1967

Bachelors	No arms could ever hold you	1964 1965
Bachelors	Ramona	1964
Bachelors	Sound of silence	1966
Bachelors	Whispering	1963
Barbra Streisand	Second hand Rose	1966
Barron Knights	Call up the groups (medley)	1964
Barron Knights	Merry gentle pops	1965 1966
Barron Knights	Pop go the workers	1965
Barron Knights	Under new management	1966 1967
Barry McGuire	Eve of destruction	1965
Barry Ryan	Elouise	1968
Beach Boys	Barbara Ann	1966
Beach Boys	Breakaway	1969
Beach Boys	Darlin'	1968
Beach Boys	Do it again	1968
Beach Boys	God only knows	1966
Beach Boys	Good vibrations	1966 1967
Beach Boys	Heroes and villains	1967
Beach Boys	I can hear music	1969
Beach Boys	I get around	1964
Beach Boys	Sloop John B	1966
Beach Boys	Then I kissed her	1967
Beatles	A hard day's night	1964
Beatles	All you need is love	1967
Beatles	Can't buy me love	1964
Beatles	Come together	1969
Beatles	Day tripper	1965 1966
Beatles	Eleanor Rigby	1966
Beatles	From me to you	1963
Beatles	Hello goodbye	1967 1968
Beatles	Help!	1965
Beatles	Hey Jude	1968
Beatles	I am the walrus	1967 1968

Artist	Song	Year
Beatles	I feel fine	1964 1965
Beatles	I want to hold your hand	1963 1964
Beatles	Lady Madonna	1968
Beatles	Love me do	1962 1963
Beatles	Magical mystery tour	1967 1968
Beatles	Paperback writer	1966
Beatles	Penny Lane	1967
Beatles	Please please me	1963
Beatles	She loves you	1963 1964
Beatles	Something	1969
Beatles	Strawberry Fields forever	1967
Beatles	The ballad of John and Yoko	1969
Beatles	Ticket to ride	1965
Beatles	We can work it out	1965 1966
Beatles	We can work it out	1965
Beatles	Yellow submarine	1966
Beatles	Your mother should know	1967 1968
Beatles & Billy Preston	Get back	1969
Bedrocks	Ob-la-di, ob-la-da	1969
Bee Gees	Don't forget to remember	1969
Bee Gees	First of May	1969
Bee Gees	I've gotta get a message to you	1968
Bee Gees	Massachusetts	1967
Bee Gees	New York mining disaster 1941	1967
Bee Gees	Words	1968
Bee Gees	World	1967 1968
Benny Hill	Gather in the mushrooms	1961
Benny Hill	Harvest of love	1963
Bern Elliott & The Fenmen	Money	1963 1964
Bernard Cribbins	Hole in the ground	1962
Bernard Cribbins	Right, said Fred	1962
Beverley Sisters	Little donkey	1960

Artist	Song	Year
Big Dee Irwin	Swinging on a star	1963 1964
Bill Haley & His Comets	Rock around the clock	1968
Billie Davis	Tell him	1963
Billy Bland	Let the little girl dance	1960
Billy Fury	A thousand stars	1961
Billy Fury	Because of love	1962
Billy Fury	Collette	1960
Billy Fury	Do you really love me too?	1964
Billy Fury	Halfway to Paradise	1961
Billy Fury	I will	1964
Billy Fury	I'd never find another you	1962
Billy Fury	I'm lost without you	1965
Billy Fury	In summer	1963
Billy Fury	In thoughts of you	1965
Billy Fury	It's only make believe	1964
Billy Fury	Jealousy	1961
Billy Fury	Last night was made for love	1962
Billy Fury	Like I've never been gone	1963
Billy Fury	Once upon a dream	1962
Billy Fury	Somebody else's girl	1963
Billy Fury	That's love	1960
Billy Fury	When will you say I love you	1963
Billy J.Kramer & The Dakotas	Bad to me	1963
Billy J.Kramer & The Dakotas	Do you want to know a secret?	1963
Billy J.Kramer & The Dakotas	From a window	1964
Billy J.Kramer & The Dakotas	I'll keep you satisfied	1963 1964
Billy J.Kramer & The Dakotas	Little children	1964
Billy J.Kramer & The Dakotas	Trains and boats and planes	1965
Billy Preston	That's the way God planned it	1969
Blue Mink	Melting pot	1969
Bob & Earl	Harlem shuffle	1969
Bob Dylan	Can you please crawl out your window?	1966
Bob Dylan	I want you	1966

Artist	Title	Year
Bob Dylan	Lay lady lay	1969
Bob Dylan	Like a rolling stone	1965
Bob Dylan	Positively 4th Street	1965 / 1966
Bob Dylan	Rainy day women no's 12 and 35	1966
Bob Dylan	Subterranean homesick blues	1965
Bob Dylan	The times they are a changin'	1965
Bob Lind	Elusive butterfly	1966
Bob Luman	Let's think about livin'	1960
Bobbie Gentry	I'll never fall in love again	1969
Bobbie Gentry	Ode to Billie Joe	1967
Bobbie Gentry & Glen Campbell	All I have to do is dream	1969
Bobby Darin	Clementine	1960
Bobby Darin	If I were a carpenter	1966
Bobby Darin	La mer (Beyond the sea)	1960
Bobby Darin	Lazy river	1961
Bobby Darin	Mack the Knife	1960
Bobby Darin	Multiplication	1962
Bobby Darin	Things	1962
Bobby Darin	You must have been a beautiful baby	1961
Bobby Goldsboro	Honey	1968
Bobby Hebb	Sunny	1966
Bobby Rydell	Forget him	1963
Bobby Rydell	Sway	1961
Bobby Rydell	Wild one	1960
Bobby Vee	A forever kind of love	1962 / 1963
Bobby Vee	How many tears	1961
Bobby Vee	More than I can say	1961
Bobby Vee	Rubber ball	1961
Bobby Vee	Run to him	1962
Bobby Vee	Sharing you	1962
Bobby Vee	Staying in	1961
Bobby Vee	Take good care of my baby	1961 / 1962
Bobby Vee	The night has a thousand eyes	1963
Bobby Vinton	Roses are red (my love)	1962
Bonzo Dog Doo-Dah Band	I'm the urban spaceman	1968 / 1969

Booker T & The MG's	Time is tight	1969
Box Tops	Cry like a baby	1968
Box Tops	The letter	1967
Brenda Lee	All alone am I	1963
Brenda Lee	As usual	1964
Brenda Lee	Here comes that feeling	1962
Brenda Lee	I wonder	1963
Brenda Lee	I'm sorry	1960
Brenda Lee	Is it true?	1964
Brenda Lee	It started all over again	1962
Brenda Lee	Let's jump the broomstick	1961
Brenda Lee	Losing you	1963
Brenda Lee	Rockin' around the Christmas tree	1962 1963
Brenda Lee	Speak to me pretty	1962
Brenda Lee	Sweet nothin's	1960
Brenton Wood	Gimme little sign	1968
Brian Hyland	Ginny come lately	1962
Brian Hyland	Itsy bitsy teeny weeny yellow polka dot bikini	1960
Brian Hyland	Sealed with a kiss	1962
Brian Poole & The Tremeloes	Candy man	1964
Brian Poole & The Tremeloes	Do you love me?	1963
Brian Poole & The Tremeloes	Someone, someone	1964
Brian Poole & The Tremeloes	Three bells	1965
Brian Poole & The Tremeloes	Twist and shout	1963
Brook Brothers	Ain't gonna wash for a week	1961
Brook Brothers	War paint	1961
Bruce Chanel	Hey! Baby	1962
Bruce Chanel	Keep on	1968
Bryan Johnson	Looking high, high, high	1960
Buddy Holly	Baby I don't care	1961
Buddy Holly	Bo Diddley	1963
Buddy Holly	Brown-eyed handsome man	1963
Buddy Holly	Reminiscing	1962
Buddy Holly	Valley of tears	1961

Artist	Song	Year
Buddy Holly	Wishing	1963
Buddy Holly & The Crickets	Don't ever change	1962
Burl Ives	A little bitty tear	1962
Burt Bacharach	Trains and boats and planes	1965
Buzz Clifford	Baby sittin' boogie	1961
Byrds	All I really want to do	1965
Byrds	Mr.Tambourine man	1965
Canned Heat	Going up the country	1969
Canned Heat	On the road again	1968
Caravelles	You don't have to be a baby to cry	1963
Carole King	It might as well rain until September	1962
Cascades	Rhythm of the rain	1963
Casuals	Jesamine	1968
Cat Stevens	A bad night	1967
Cat Stevens	I'm gonna get me a gun	1967
Cat Stevens	Matthew and son	1967
Chantays	Pipeline	1963
Charlie Drake	Mr.Custer	1960
Charlie Drake	My boomerang won't come back	1961
Cher	All I really want to do	1965
Cher	Bang bang (my baby shot me down)	1966
Chicken Shack	I'd rather go blind	1969
Chiffons	He's so fine	1963
Chris Andrews	To whom it concerns	1965 1966
Chris Andrews	Yesterday man	1965 1966
Chris Farlowe	Out of time	1966
Chris Montez	Let's dance	1962 1963
Chris Montez	Some kinda fun	1963
Chris Montez	The more I see you	1966
Chris Sandford	Not too little - not too much	1963 1964
Chubby Checker	Dancin' party	1962
Chubby Checker	Let's twist again	1962
Chubby Checker	The twist	1962

Chuck Berry	Let it rock	1963
Chuck Berry	Memphis Tennessee	1963
Chuck Berry	No particluar place to go	1964
Cilla Black	A fool am I	1966
Cilla Black	Alfie	1966
Cilla Black	Anyone who had a heart	1964
Cilla Black	Conversations	1969
Cilla Black	Don't answer me	1966
Cilla Black	It's for you	1964
Cilla Black	I've been wrong before	1965
Cilla Black	Love's just a broken heart	1966
Cilla Black	Step inside love	1968
Cilla Black	Surround yourself with sorrow	1969
Cilla Black	You're my world	1964
Cilla Black	You've lost that lovin' feelin'	1965
Clarence 'Frogman' Henry	(I don't know why I love you) but I do	1961
Clarence 'Frogman' Henry	You always hurt the one you love	1961
Cleo Laine	You'll answer to me	1961
Cliff Bennett & The Rebel Rousers	Got to get you into my life	1966
Cliff Bennett & The Rebel Rousers	One way love	1964
Cliff Richard	A girl like you	1961
Cliff Richard	All my love	1967 1968
Cliff Richard	Bachelor boy	1962 1963
Cliff Richard	Big ship	1969
Cliff Richard	Blue turns to grey	1966
Cliff Richard	Congratulations	1968
Cliff Richard	Constantly	1964
Cliff Richard	Do you want to dance	1962
Cliff Richard	Don't talk to him	1963 1964
Cliff Richard	Gee whizz it's you	1961
Cliff Richard	Good times	1969
Cliff Richard	I could easily fall	1964 1965
Cliff Richard	I love you	1960 1961

Artist	Song	Year
Cliff Richard	I'm looking out the window	1962
Cliff Richard	I'm the lonely one	1964
Cliff Richard	It'll be me	1962
Cliff Richard	It's all in the game	1963
Cliff Richard	It's all over	1967
Cliff Richard	Lucky lips	1963
Cliff Richard	Nine times out of ten	1960
Cliff Richard	On my word	1965
Cliff Richard	On the beach	1964
Cliff Richard	Please don't tease	1960
Cliff Richard	Summer holiday	1963
Cliff Richard	The day I met Marie	1967
Cliff Richard	The minute you're gone	1965
Cliff Richard	The next time	1962 1963
Cliff Richard	The twelfth of never	1964
Cliff Richard	The young ones	1962
Cliff Richard	Throw down a line	1969
Cliff Richard	Time drags by	1966
Cliff Richard	Visions	1966
Cliff Richard	When the girl in your arms is the girl in your heart	1961
Cliff Richard	Wind me up (let me go)	1965 1966
Cliff Richard	With the eyes of a child	1969
Cliff Richard	Theme for a dream	1961
Cliff Richard & The Shadows	A voice in the wilderness	1960
Cliff Richard & The Shadows	Bongo blues	1960
Cliff Richard & The Shadows	Easily fall in love with you	1960
Cliff Richard & The Shadows	In the country	1967
Cliff Richard & The Shadows	Love	1960
Cliff Richard & The Shadows	The shrine on the second floor	1960
Cliff Richard & The Shadows	Travellin' light	1960
Clodagh Rodgers	Come back and shake me	1969
Clodagh Rodgers	Goodnight midnight	1969

Artist	Song	Year
Connie Francis	Among my souvenirs	1960
Connie Francis	Baby Roo	1961
Connie Francis	Breakin' a brand new broken heart	1961
Connie Francis	Everybody's somebody's fool	1960
Connie Francis	Mama	1960
Connie Francis	Many tears ago	1961
Connie Francis	My heart has a mind of its own	1960 1961
Connie Francis	Robot man	1960
Connie Francis	Together	1961
Connie Francis	V.A.C.A.T.I.O.N.	1962
Connie Francis	Where the boys are	1961
Connie Stevens	Sixteen reasons	1960
Craig Douglas	A hundred pounds of clay	1961
Craig Douglas	Oh, lonesome me	1962
Craig Douglas	Our favourite melodies	1962
Craig Douglas	Pretty blue eyes	1960
Craig Douglas	The heart of a teenage girl	1960
Craig Douglas	Time	1961
Craig Douglas	When my little girl is smiling	1962
Crazy Elephant	Gimme, gimme, good loving	1969
Crazy World Of Arthur Brown	Fire!	1968
Cream	Badge	1969
Cream	I feel free	1967
Cream	Strange brew	1967
Creedence Clearwater Revival	Bad moon rising	1969
Creedence Clearwater Revival	Green river	1969
Creedence Clearwater Revival	Proud Mary	1969
Crickets	My little girl	1963
Crispian St.Peters	The Pied Piper	1966
Crispian St.Peters	You were on my mind	1966
Crosby, Still & Nash	Marrakesh Express	1969
Crystals	Da doo ron ron	1963
Crystals	He's a rebel	1963
Crystals	Then he kissed me	1963
Cufflinks	Tracy	1969

Cupid's Inspiration	Yesterday has gone	1968
Dakotas	The cruel sea	1963
Danny Williams	Jeannie	1962
Danny Williams	Moon river	1961 1962
Danny Williams	Wonderful world of the young	1962
Dave Berry	Little things	1965
Dave Berry	Mama	1966
Dave Berry	The crying game	1964
Dave Berry & The Cruisers	Memphis Tennessee	1963
Dave Brubeck	Unsquare dance	1962
Dave Brubeck Quartet	Take five	1961
Dave Clark Five	Bits and pieces	1964
Dave Clark Five	Can't you see that she's mine	1964
Dave Clark Five	Catch us if you can	1965
Dave Clark Five	Come home	1965
Dave Clark Five	Everybody knows	1967 1968
Dave Clark Five	Glad all over	1963 1964
Dave Clark Five	Good old rock 'n' roll	1969
Dave Clark Five	The red balloon	1968
Dave Davies	Death of a clown	1967
Dave Davies	Susannah's still alive	1968
Dave Dee, Dozy, Beaky Mick & Tich	Bend it!	1966
Dave Dee, Dozy, Beaky Mick & Tich	Hideaway	1966
Dave Dee, Dozy, Beaky Mick & Tich	Hold tight!	1966
Dave Dee, Dozy, Beaky Mick & Tich	Save me	1966 1967
Dave Dee, Dozy, Beaky, Mick & Tich	Last night in Soho	1968
Dave Dee, Dozy, Beaky, Mick & Tich	Okay!	1967
Dave Dee, Dozy, Beaky, Mick & Tich	The legend of Xanadu	1968
Dave Dee, Dozy, Beaky, Mick & Tich	The wreck of the Antoinette	1968

Artist	Song	Year
Dave Dee, Dozy, Beaky, Mick & Tich	Touch me, touch me	1967
Dave Dee, Dozy, Beaky, Mick & Tich	Zabadak!	1967
David & Jonathan	Lovers of the world unite	1966
David & Jonathan	Michelle	1966
David Bowie	Space oddity	1969
Dean Martin	Everybody loves somebody sometime	1964
Dean Martin	Gentle on my mind	1969
Del Shannon	Hats off to Larry	1961
Del Shannon	Hey! Little girl	1962
Del Shannon	Keep searchin' (we'll follow the sun)	1965
Del Shannon	Little town flirt	1963
Del Shannon	Runaway	1961
Del Shannon	So long baby	1961 1962
Del Shannon	The Swiss maid	1962 1963
Del Shannon	Two kinds of teardrops	1963
Dells	I can sing a rainbow - love is blue (medley)	1969
Des O'Connor	1-2-3 O'Leary	1968 1969
Des O'Connor	Careless hands	1967 1968
Des O'Connor	Dick-a-dum-dum (King's Road)	1969
Des O'Connor	I pretend	1968
Des O'Connor	Loneliness	1969
Desmond Dekker & The Aces	007 (Shanty town)	1967
Desmond Dekker & The Aces	It miek	1969
Desmond Dekker & The Aces	The Israelites	1969
Diana Ross & The Supremes	I'm living in shame	1969
Diana Ross & The Supremes	In and out of love	1967 1968
Diana Ross & The Supremes	Love child	1968 1969

Artist	Title	Year
Diana Ross & The Supremes	Reflections	1967
Diana Ross & The Supremes & The Temptations	I second that emotion	1969
Diana Ross & The Supremes & The Temptations	I'm gonna make you love me	1969
Dion	Runaround Sue	1961
Dion & The Belmonts	The wanderer	1962
Dionne Warwick	Do you know the way to San Jose?	1968
Dionne Warwick	Walk on by	1964
Dionne Warwick	You'll never get to heaven (if you break my heart)	1964
Don Gibson	Sea of heartbreak	1961
Don Partridge	Blue eyes	1968
Don Partridge	Rosie	1968
Donald Peers	Please don't go	1969
Donovan	Catch the wind	1965
Donovan	Colours	1965
Donovan	Hurdy Gurdy Man	1968
Donovan	Jennifer Juniper	1968
Donovan	Mellow yellow	1967
Donovan	Sunshine Superman	1966 1967
Donovan	There is a mountain	1967
Donovan & Jeff Beck Group	Goo Goo Barabajagal (Love is hot)	1969
Doors	Hello I love you	1968
Dora Bryan	All I want for Christmas is a Beatle	1964
Doris Day	Move over darling	1964
Dorothy Provine	Don't bring Lulu	1962
Drifters	Dance with me	1960
Drifters	Save the last dance for me	1960 1961
Duane Eddy	Ballad of Paladin	1962
Duane Eddy	Because they're young	1960
Duane Eddy	Bonnie came back	1960
Duane Eddy	Deep in the heart of Texas	1962
Duane Eddy	Kommotion	1960

Duane Eddy	Pepe	1961
Duane Eddy	Ring of fire	1961
Duane Eddy	Shazam	1960
Duane Eddy	Some kind-a-earthquake	1960
Duane Eddy	Theme from Dixie	1961
Duane Eddy & The Rebelettes	Dance with the guitar man	1962 1963
Dubliners	Black velvet band	1967
Dubliners	Seven drunken nights	1967
Dusty Springfield	All I see is you	1966
Dusty Springfield	Going back	1966
Dusty Springfield	I close my eyes and count to ten	1968
Dusty Springfield	I just don't know what to do with myself	1964
Dusty Springfield	I only want to be with you	1963 1964
Dusty Springfield	I'll try anything	1967
Dusty Springfield	In the middle of nowhere	1965
Dusty Springfield	Little by little	1966
Dusty Springfield	Losing you	1964
Dusty Springfield	Some of your lovin'	1965
Dusty Springfield	Son of a preacher man	1968 1969
Dusty Springfield	Stay awhile	1964
Dusty Springfield	You don't have to say you love me	1966
Easybeats	Friday on my mind	1966 1967
Easybeats	Hello, how are you ?	1968
Eddie Cochran	Three steps to heaven	1960
Eddie Cochran	Weekend	1961
Eddie Floyd	Knock on wood	1967
Eddy Arnold	Make the world go away	1966
Eden Kane	Boys cry	1964
Eden Kane	Forget me not	1962
Eden Kane	Get lost	1961
Eden Kane	I don't know why	1962
Eden Kane	Well I ask you	1961
Edwin Hawkins Singers	Oh happy day	1969
Edwin Starr	Headline news	1969
Edwin Starr	Stop her on sight	1969

Ella Fitzgerald	Mack the Knife	1960
Elmer Bernstein	Staccato's theme	1960
Elvis Presley	(Marie's the name of) His latest flame	1961 1962
Elvis Presley	(You're the) devil in disguise	1963
Elvis Presley	A mess of blues	1960
Elvis Presley	Ain't that lovin' you baby	1964
Elvis Presley	All that I am	1966
Elvis Presley	Are you lonesome tonight?	1961
Elvis Presley	Blue Christmas	1964 1965
Elvis Presley	Bossa Nova baby	1963
Elvis Presley	Can't help falling in love	1962
Elvis Presley	Crying in the chapel	1965
Elvis Presley	Do the clam	1965
Elvis Presley	Good luck charm	1962
Elvis Presley	Guitar man	1968
Elvis Presley	I feel so bad	1961
Elvis Presley	If every day was like Christmas	1966 1967
Elvis Presley	If I can dream	1969
Elvis Presley	In the ghetto	1969
Elvis Presley	It's now or never	1960 1961
Elvis Presley	Kiss me quick	1964
Elvis Presley	Kissin' cousins	1964
Elvis Presley	Little sister	1961 1962
Elvis Presley	Love letters	1966
Elvis Presley	One broken heart for sale	1963
Elvis Presley	Return to sender	1962 1963
Elvis Presley	Rock-a-hula baby	1962
Elvis Presley	She's not you	1962
Elvis Presley	Stuck on you	1960
Elvis Presley	Such a night	1964
Elvis Presley	Surrender	1961
Elvis Presley	Suspicious minds	1969
Elvis Presley	Tell me why	1965
Elvis Presley	U.S.Male	1968
Elvis Presley	Viva Las Vegas	1964

Artist	Title	Year
Elvis Presley	Wild in the country	1961
Elvis Presley	Wooden heart	1961
Emile Ford & The Checkmates	Counting teardrops	1960 1961
Emile Ford & The Checkmates	On a slow boat to China	1960
Emile Ford & The Checkmates	Them there eyes	1960
Emile Ford & The Checkmates	What do you want to make those eyes at me for?	1960
Emile Ford & The Checkmates	You'll never know what you're missing	1960
Engelbert Humperdinck	Release me	1967
Engelbert Humperdinck	The last waltz	1967 1968
Engelbert Humperdinck	There goes my everything	1967
Engelbert Humperdinck	I'm a better man	1969
Engelbert Humperdinck	The way it used to be	1969
Engelbert Humperdinck	Winter world of love	1969
Englebert Humperdinck	A man without love	1968
Englebert Humperdinck	Am I that easy to forget?	1968
Englebert Humperdinck	Les bicyclettes de Belsize	1968
Equals	Baby come back	1968
Equals	Viva Bobby Joe	1969
Eric Burdon	San Franciscan nights	1967
Eric Burdon & The Animals	Good times	1967
Eric Burdon & The Animals	Help me girl	1966
Ernie Fields & His Orchestra	In the mood	1960
Esther & Abi Ofarim	Cinderella Rockefella	1968
Esther & Abi Ofarim	One more dance	1968
Everly Brothers	Cathy's clown	1960
Everly Brothers	Don't blame me	1961
Everly Brothers	Ebony eyes	1961
Everly Brothers	How can I meet her	1962
Everly Brothers	I'll do my crying in the rain	1962
Everly Brothers	Let it be me	1960
Everly Brothers	Like strangers	1961
Everly Brothers	Love is strange	1965

Artist	Song	Year
Everly Brothers	Lucille	1960
Everly Brothers	Muskrat	1961
Everly Brothers	No one can make my sunshine smile	1962
Everly Brothers	So sad	1960
Everly Brothers	Temptation	1961
Everly Brothers	The price of love	1965
Everly Brothers	Walk right back	1961
Everly Brothers	When will I be loved	1960
Eydie Gorme	Yes my darling daughter	1962
Family Dogg	Way of life	1969
Fats Domino	Be my guest	1960
Fats Domino	Country boy	1960
Fats Domino	Walking to New Orleans	1960
Felice Taylor	I feel love coming on	1967
Ferrante & Teicher	Theme from 'Exodus'	1961
Fleetwood Mac	Albatross	1968 / 1969
Fleetwood Mac	Man of the world	1969
Fleetwood Mac	Oh well	1969
Flower Pot Men	Let's go to San Francisco	1967
Floyd Cramer	On the rebound	1961
Fontella Bass	Rescue me	1965 / 1966
Fortunes	Here it comes again	1965
Fortunes	This golden ring	1966
Fortunes	You've got your troubles	1965
Foundations	Baby now that I've found you	1967
Foundations	Back on my feet again	1968
Foundations	Build me up buttercup	1968 / 1969
Foundations	In the bad, bad old days	1969
Four Pennies	Black girl	1964
Four Pennies	I found out the hard way	1964
Four Pennies	Juliet	1964
Four Pennies	Until it's time for you to go	1965
Four Seasons	Big girls don't cry	1963
Four Seasons	I've got you under my skin	1966
Four Seasons	Let's hang on	1965 / 1966

Artist	Song	Year
Four Seasons	Opus 17 (Don't you worry 'bout me)	1966
Four Seasons	Rag doll	1964
Four Seasons	Sherry	1962
Four Seasons	Walk like a man	1963
Four Tops	Bernadette	1967
Four Tops	Do what you gotta do	1969
Four Tops	If I were a carpenter	1968
Four Tops	Reach out I'll be there	1966 1967
Four Tops	Seven rooms of gloom	1967
Four Tops	Standing in the shadows of love	1967
Four Tops	Walk away Renee	1967 1968
Four Tops	What is a man?	1969
Fourmost	A little loving	1964
Fourmost	Hello little girl	1963
Fourmost	I'm in love	1964
Francoise Hardy	All over the world	1965
Frank Ifield	Confessin' (that I love you)	1963
Frank Ifield	Don't blame me	1964
Frank Ifield	I remember you	1962
Frank Ifield	Lovesick blues	1962 1963
Frank Ifield	Nobody's darlin' but mine	1963
Frank Ifield	The wayward wind	1963
Frank Sinatra	Granada	1961
Frank Sinatra	Love's been good to me	1969
Frank Sinatra	My way	1969
Frank Sinatra	Nice 'n' easy	1960
Frank Sinatra	Ol' MacDonald	1960 1961
Frank Sinatra	River, stay 'way from my door	1960
Frank Sinatra	Strangers in the night	1966
Frank Sinatra & Sammy Davis Jr.	Me and my shadow	1963
Frankie Avalon	Why	1960
Frankie Laine	Rawhide	1960
Frankie McBride	Five little fingers	1967
Frankie Vaughan	Hello, Dolly!	1964
Frankie Vaughan	Loop-de-loop	1963

Artist	Song	Year
Frankie Vaughan	There must be a way	1967 1968
Frankie Vaughan	Tower of strength	1961 1962
Freddie & The Dreamers	I love you baby	1964
Freddie & The Dreamers	I understand	1964 1965
Freddie & The Dreamers	If you gotta make a fool of somebody	1963
Freddie & The Dreamers	I'm tellin' you now	1963
Freddie & The Dreamers	Over you	1964
Freddie & The Dreamers	You were made for me	1963 1964
Freddy Cannon	Palisades Park	1962
Freddy Cannon	The urge	1960
Freddy Cannon	Way down yonder in New Orleans	1960
Gary Mills	Look for a star	1960
Gary Puckett & The Union Gap	Lady Willpower	1968
Gary Puckett & The Union Gap	Young girl	1968
Gary U.S.Bonds	New Orleans	1961
Gary U.S.Bonds	Quarter to three	1961
G-Clefs	I understand (just how you feel)	1961 1962
Gene Pitney	Backstage	1966
Gene Pitney	I must be seeing things	1965
Gene Pitney	I'm gonna be strong	1964 1965
Gene Pitney	Just one smile	1966 1967
Gene Pitney	Looking through the eyes of love	1965
Gene Pitney	Nobody needs your love	1966
Gene Pitney	Princess in rags	1965 1966
Gene Pitney	Something's gotten hold of my heart	1967 1968
Gene Pitney	Somewhere in the country	1968
Gene Pitney	That girl belongs to yesterday	1964

Artist	Title	Year
Gene Pitney	Twenty four hours from Tulsa	1963 1964
Gene Vincent	My heart	1960
Gene Vincent	Pistol packin' mama	1960
Georgie Fame	Because I love you	1967
Georgie Fame	Peaceful	1969
Georgie Fame	Sitting in the park	1967
Georgie Fame	Sunny	1966
Georgie Fame	The ballad of Bonnie and Clyde	1968
Georgie Fame	Yeh yeh	1964 1965
Georgie Fame & The Blue Flames	Getaway	1966
Gerry & The Paceakers	Ferry 'cross the Mersey	1965
Gerry & The Paceakers	I'll be there	1965
Gerry & The Pacemakers	Don't let the sun catch you crying	1964
Gerry & The Pacemakers	How do you do it?	1963
Gerry & The Pacemakers	I like it	1963
Gerry & The Pacemakers	I'm the one	1964
Gerry & The Pacemakers	You'll never walk alone	1963 1964
Gigliola Cinquetti	Non ho l'eta per amarti	1964
Gladys Knight & The Pips	Take me in your arms and love me	1967
Glen Campbell	Galveston	1969
Glen Campbell	Wichita lineman	1969
Graham Bonney	Supergirl	1966
Gun	Race with the devil	1968 1969
Guy Mitchell	Heartaches by the number	1960
Hank Locklin	Please help me I'm falling	1960
Hank Locklin	We're gonna go fishin'	1963
Harry J. & The All Stars	The Liquidator	1969
Harry Secombe	If I ruled the world	1963
Harry Secombe	This is my song	1967
Hayley Mills	Let's get together	1961
Hedgehoppers Anonymous	It's good news week	1965
Heinz	Just like Eddie	1963
Helen Shapiro	Don't treat me like a child	1961

Artist	Title	Year
Helen Shapiro	Little Miss Lonely	1962
Helen Shapiro	Tell me what he said	1962
Helen Shapiro	Walking back to happiness	1961 1962
Helen Shapiro	You don't know	1961
Helmut Zacharias	Tokyo melody	1964
Henry Mancini & His Orchestra	How soon	1964
Herb Alpert	This guy's in love with you	1968
Herb Alpert & The Tijuana Brass	Spanish flea	1966
Herd	From the underworld	1967
Herd	I don't want our loving to die	1968
Herd	Paradise lost	1968
Herman's Hermits	A must to avoid	1966
Herman's Hermits	I can take or leave your loving	1968
Herman's Hermits	I'm into something good	1964
Herman's Hermits	Just a little bit better	1965
Herman's Hermits	My sentimental friend	1969
Herman's Hermits	No milk today	1966
Herman's Hermits	Show me girl	1964
Herman's Hermits	Silhouettes	1965
Herman's Hermits	Sleepy Joe	1968
Herman's Hermits	Something's happening	1969
Herman's Hermits	Sunshine girl	1968
Herman's Hermits	There's a kind of hush	1967
Herman's Hermits	This door swings both ways	1966
Herman's Hermits	Wonderful world	1965
Herman's Hermits	You won't be leavin'	1966
Highwaymen	Michael	1961
Hollies	Bus stop	1966
Hollies	Carrie-Anne	1967
Hollies	He ain't heavy…he's my brother	1969
Hollies	Here I go again	1964
Hollies	I can't let go	1966
Hollies	If I needed someone	1966
Hollies	I'm alive	1965
Hollies	Jennifer Eccles	1968
Hollies	Just one look	1964
Hollies	King Midas in reverse	1967
Hollies	Listen to me	1968

Hollies	Look through any window	1965
Hollies	On a carousel	1967
Hollies	Searchin'	1963
Hollies	Sorry Suzanne	1969
Hollies	Stay	1963 1964
Hollies	Stop stop stop	1966
Hollies	We're through	1964
Hollies	Yes I will	1965
Honeybus	I can't let Maggie go	1968
Honeycombs	Have I the right?	1964
Honeycombs	That's the way	1965
Horst Jankowski	Walk in the Black Forest	1965
Hugo Montenegro	The good, the bad, and the ugly	1968 1969
Humble Pie	Natural born boogie	1969
Ike & Tina Turner	A love like yours	1966
Ike & Tina Turner	River deep, mountain high	1966
Isley Brothers	Behind a painted smile	1969
Isley Brothers	I guess I'll always love you	1969
Isley Brothers	Put yourself in my place	1969
Isley Brothers	This old heart of mine	1968 1969
Ivy League	Funny how love can be	1965
Ivy League	Tossing and turning	1965
Jack Scott	What in the world's come over you?	1960
Jackie	White horses	1968
Jackie Trent	Where are you now (my love)	1965
Jackie Wilson	(Your love keeps lifting me) higher and higher	1969
James Brown	It's a man's man's man's world	1966
Jane Birkin & Serge Gainsbourg	Je t'aime....moi non plus	1969
Jeannie C.Riley	Harper Valley P.T.A.	1968
Jeff Beck	Hi ho silver lining	1967
Jerry Lee Lewis	What'd I say	1961
Jerry Lordan	Who could be bluer?	1960
Jess Conrad	Mystery girl	1961
Jet Harris	Theme from 'The Man With The Golden Arm'	1962

Artist	Title	Year
Jet Harris & Tony Meehan	Applejack	1963
Jet Harris & Tony Meehan	Diamonds	1963
Jet Harris & Tony Meehan	Scarlett O'Hara	1963
Jethro Tull	Living in the past	1969
Jethro Tull	Sweet dream	1969
Jim Reeves	But you love me Daddy	1969
Jim Reeves	Distant drums	1966 1967
Jim Reeves	He'll have to go	1960
Jim Reeves	I love you because	1964
Jim Reeves	I won't come in while he's there	1967
Jim Reeves	I won't forget you	1964
Jim Reeves	Is it really over	1965
Jim Reeves	It hurts so much (to see you go)	1965
Jim Reeves	Not until the next time	1965
Jim Reeves	There's a heartache following me	1964 1965
Jim Reeves	Welcome to my world	1963
Jim Reeves	When two worlds collide	1969
Jim Reeves	You're the only good thing (that happened to me)	1961 1962
Jimi Hendrix Experience	All along the watchtower	1968
Jimi Hendrix Experience	Burning of the midnight lamp	1967
Jimi Hendrix Experience	Hey Joe	1967
Jimi Hendrix Experience	Purple haze	1967
Jimi Hendrix Experience	The wind cries Mary	1967
Jimmy Cliff	Wonderful world, beautiful people	1969
Jimmy Crawford	I love how you love me	1961
Jimmy Dean	Big bad John	1961 1962
Jimmy Jones	Good timin'	1960
Jimmy Jones	Handy man	1960
Jimmy Justice	Ain't that funny	1962
Jimmy Justice	Spanish Harlem	1962
Jimmy Justice	When my little girl is smiling	1962
Jimmy Rodgers	English country garden	1962
Jimmy Ruffin	What becomes of the broken-hearted ?	1966 1967
Jimmy Young	Miss you	1963
Joan Baez	There but for fortune	1965
Joe Brown	A picture of you	1962

Artist	Song	Year
Joe Brown	It only took a minute	1962 1963
Joe Brown	That's what love will do	1963
Joe Cocker	Delta lady	1969
Joe Cocker	With a little help from my friends	1968
Joe Dolan	Make me an island	1969
Joe Dolan	Teresa	1969
Joe Loss & His Orchestra	Must be Madison	1962
Joe Loss & His Orchestra	Theme from 'Maigret'	1962
Joe South	Games people play	1969
John Barry Orchestra	Theme from 'James Bond'	1962
John Barry Seven	Hit and miss	1960
John Barry Seven	Walk don't run	1960
John D.Loudermilk	The language of love	1962
John Fred & The Playboy Band	Judy in disguise (with glasses)	1968
John Lennon & Yoko One With The Plastic Ono Band	Cold turkey	1969
John Lennon & Yoko One With The Plastic Ono Band	Give peace a chance	1969
John Leyton	Johnny remember me	1961
John Leyton	Lonely city	1962
John Leyton	Son, this is she	1962
John Leyton	Wild wind	1961
John Rowles	Hush…not a word to Mary	1968
John Rowles	If I only had time	1968
Johnny & The Hurricanes	Beatnik fly	1960
Johnny & The Hurricanes	Down yonder	1960
Johnny & The Hurricanes	Ja-da	1961
Johnny & The Hurricanes	Red River rock	1960
Johnny & The Hurricanes	Reveille rock	1960
Johnny & The Hurricanes	Rocking goose	1960 1961
Johnny Burnette	Dreamin'	1960 1961
Johnny Burnette	Little boy sad	1961
Johnny Burnette	You're sixteen	1961
Johnny Cash	A boy named Sue	1969
Johnny Dankworth	African waltz	1961

Artist	Title	Year
Johnny Johnson & His Bandwagon	Breakin' down the walls of heartache	1968 1969
Johnny Keating Orchestra	Theme from 'Z-Cars'	1962
Johnny Kidd & The Pirates	Hungry for love	1963
Johnny Kidd & The Pirates	I'll never get over you	1963
Johnny Kidd & The Pirates	Shakin' all over	1960
Johnny Mann Singers	Up, up and away	1967
Johnny Mathis	Misty	1960
Johnny Mathis	My love for you	1960 1961
Johnny Nash	Cupid	1969
Johnny Nash	Hold me tight	1968
Johnny Nash	You got soul	1969
Johnny Preston	Cradle of love	1960
Johnny Preston	Feel so fine	1960
Johnny Preston	Running bear	1960
Johnny Spence	Theme from 'Dr.Kildare'	1962
Johnny Tillotson	Poetry in motion	1960 1961
Jonathan King	Everyone's gone to the moon	1965
Jose Feliciano	Light my fire	1968
Jr.Walker & The Allstars	Road runner	1969
Jr.Walker & The Allstars	What does it take (to win your love)?	1969
Judy Clay & William Bell	Private number	1968 1969
Julie Driscoll, Brian Auger & The Trinity	This wheel's on fire	1968
Julie Rogers	Like a child	1965
Julie Rogers	The wedding	1964
Karen Young	Nobody's child	1969
Karl Denver	A little love, a little kiss	1962
Karl Denver	Marcheta	1961
Karl Denver	Mexicali Rose	1961
Karl Denver	Never goodbye	1962
Karl Denver	Still	1963
Karl Denver	Wimoweh	1962

Kasenetz-Katz Singing Orchestral Circus	Quick Joey Small (run Joey run)	1969
Kathy Kirby	Dance on!	1963
Kathy Kirby	Let me go, lover	1964
Kathy Kirby	Secret love	1963 1964
Kathy Kirby	You're the one	1964
Kaye Sisters	Paper roses	1960
Keely Smith	You're breakin' my heart	1965
Keith West	Excerpt from 'A Teenage Opera'	1967
Ken Dodd	Let me cry on your shoulder	1967
Ken Dodd	Love is like a violin	1960
Ken Dodd	More than love	1966
Ken Dodd	Promises	1966
Ken Dodd	Tears	1965 1966
Ken Dodd	The river	1965 1966
Ken Thorne	Theme from 'The Legion's Last Patrol'	1963
Kenny Ball & His Jazzmen	March of the Siamese children	1962
Kenny Ball & His Jazzmen	Midnight in Moscow	1961 1962
Kenny Ball & His Jazzmen	Samantha	1961
Kenny Ball & His Jazzmen	So do I	1962
Kenny Ball & His Jazzmen	Sukiyaki	1963
Kenny Ball & His Jazzmen	The green leaves of summer	1962
Kenny Lynch	Up on the roof	1963
Kenny Lynch	You can never stop me loving you	1963
Kenny Rogers & The First Edition	Ruby, don't take your love to town	1969
Ketty Lester	Love letters	1962
King Brothers	76 Trombones	1961
King Brothers	Mais oui	1960
King Brothers	Standing on the corner	1960

Kinks	All day and all of the night	1964 1965
Kinks	Autumn Almanac	1967
Kinks	Days	1968
Kinks	Dead end street	1966 1967
Kinks	Dedicated follower of fashion	1966
Kinks	Everybody's gonna be happy	1965
Kinks	See my friend	1965
Kinks	Set me free	1965
Kinks	Sunny afternoon	1966
Kinks	Till the end of the day	1965 1966
Kinks	Tired of waiting for you	1965
Kinks	Waterloo sunset	1967
Kinks	You really got me	1964
Kyu Sakamoto	Sukiyaki	1963
Lance Fortune	Be mine	1960
Laurie Johnson Orchestra	Sucu sucu	1961
Leapy Lee	Little arrows	1968
Lee Dorsey	Holy cow	1966 1967
Lee Dorsey	Working in the coal mine	1966
Lemon Pipers	Green tambourine	1968
Len Barry	1,2,3	1965 1966
Len Barry	Like a baby	1966
Leroy Van Dyke	Walk on by	1962
Lesley Gore	It's my party	1963
Lesley Gore	Maybe I know	1964
Linda Scott	I've told every little star	1961
Little Eva	Let's turkey trot	1963
Little Eva	The loco-motion	1962
Little Richard	Bama lama bama loo	1964
Little Tony	Too good	1960
Long John Baldry	Let the heartaches begin	1967 1968
Long John Baldry	Mexico	1968
Lonnie Donegan	Have a drink on me	1961
Lonnie Donegan	I wanna go home	1960

Lonnie Donegan	Lively	1960 1961
Lonnie Donegan	Lorelei	1960
Lonnie Donegan	Lumbered	1961
Lonnie Donegan	Michael, row the boat	1961
Lonnie Donegan	My old man's a dustman	1960
Lonnie Donegan	Pick a bale of cotton	1962
Lonnie Donegan	The Comancheros	1962
Lonnie Donegan	The party's over	1962
Los Bravos	Black is black	1966
Los Bravos	I don't care	1966
Los Indios Tagajaras	Maria Elena	1963 1964
Lou Christie	I'm gonna make you mine	1969
Lou Christie	Lightning strikes	1966
Louis Armstrong	Cabaret	1968
Louis Armstrong	Hello, Dolly!	1964
Louis Armstrong	What a wonderful world	1968
Louise Cordet	I'm just a baby	1962
Love Affair	A day without love	1968
Love Affair	Bringing on back the good times	1969
Love Affair	Everlasting love	1968
Love Affair	One road	1969
Love Affair	Rainbow valley	1968
Love Scultpture	Sabre dance	1968 1969
Lovin' Spoonful	Daydream	1966
Lovin' Spoonful	Summer in the city	1966
Lulu	Boom bang-a-bang	1969
Lulu	Boy	1968
Lulu	I'm a tiger	1968 1969
Lulu	Leave a little love	1965
Lulu	Let's pretend	1967
Lulu	Me, the peaceful heart	1968
Lulu	The boat that I row	1967
Lulu & The Luvvers	Shout	1964
Malcolm Roberts	Love is all	1969
Malcolm Roberts	May I have the next dream with you?	1968 1969
Mama Cass	Dream a little dream of me	1968

Mama Cass	It's getting better	1969
Mamas & Papas	Creeque Alley	1967
Mamas & Papas	Dedicated to the one I love	1967
Mamas & Papas	I saw her again	1966
Mamas & Papas	Monday Monday	1966
Manfred Mann	5-4-3-2-1	1964
Manfred Mann	Come tomorrow	1965
Manfred Mann	Do wah diddy diddy	1964
Manfred Mann	Fox on the run	1969
Manfred Mann	Ha! Ha! Said the clown	1967
Manfred Mann	Hubble bubble (toil and trouble)	1964
Manfred Mann	If you gotta go, go now	1965
Manfred Mann	Just like a woman	1966
Manfred Mann	My name is Jack	1968
Manfred Mann	Oh no not my baby	1965
Manfred Mann	Pretty flamingo	1966
Manfred Mann	Ragamuffin man	1969
Manfred Mann	Semi-detached suburban Mr.James	1966
Manfred Mann	Sha la la	1964
Manfred Mann	The Mighty Quinn	1968
Marbles	Only one woman	1968
Marcello Minerbi	Zorba's dance	1965
Marcels	Blue moon	1961
Marianne Faithfull	As tears go by	1964
Marianne Faithfull	Come and stay with me	1965
Marianne Faithfull	Summer nights	1965
Marianne Faithfull	This little bird	1965
Mark Wynter	Go away little girl	1963
Mark Wynter	Image of a girl	1960
Mark Wynter	It's almost tomorrow	1963
Mark Wynter	Venus in blue jeans	1962
Marmalade	Baby make it soon	1969
Marmalade	Lovin' things	1968
Marmalade	Ob-la-di, ob-la-da	1968 1969
Martha Reeves & The Vandellas	Dancing in the street	1969
Marty Robbins	Devil woman	1962 1963
Marty Robbins	El Paso	1960

Artist	Song	Year
Marty Wilde	Bad boy	1960
Marty Wilde	Jezebel	1962
Marty Wilde	Little girl	1961
Marty Wilde	Rubber ball	1961
Marv Johnson	I'll pick a rose for my rose	1969
Marv Johnson	You got what it takes	1960
Marvelettes	When you're young and in love	1967
Marvin Gaye	I heard it through the grapevine	1969
Marvin Gaye	Too busy thinking 'bout my baby	1969
Marvin Gaye & Kim Weston	It takes two	1967
Marvin Gaye & Tammi Terrell	The onion song	1969
Marvin Gaye & Tammi Terrell	You're all I need to get by	1968
Mary Hopkin	Goodbye	1969
Mary Hopkin	Those were the days	1968
Mary Wells	My guy	1964
Mason Williams	Classical gas	1968
Matt Monro	From Russia with love	1963
Matt Monro	My kind of girl	1961
Matt Monro	Portrait of my love	1961
Matt Monro	Softly as I leave you	1962
Matt Monro	Walk away	1964
Matt Monro	Yesterday	1965
Maureen Evans	Like I do	1962 1963
Maurice Williams & The Zodiacs	Stay	1961
Max Bygraves	Fings ain't wot they used to be	1960
Max Bygraves	Jingle bell rock	1960
Max Harris	Gurney Slade	1960 1961
Max Romeo	Wet dream	1969
McCoys	Hang on Sloopy	1965
Mel Torme	Coming home baby	1963
Merseybeats	Don't turn around	1964
Merseybeats	I think of you	1964
Merseybeats	Wishin' and hopin'	1964
Merseys	Sorrow	1966
Michael Cox	Angela Jones	1960

Michael Holliday	Starry eyed	1960
Migil 5	Mockin' Bird Hill	1964
Mike Berry & The Outlaws	Don't you think it's time ?	1963
Mike Preston	Marry me	1961
Mike Sammes Singers	Somewhere my love	1967
Mike Sarne	Will I what?	1962
Mike Sarne & Wendy Richard	Come outside	1962
Miki & Griff	A little bitty tear	1962
Millie	My boy lollipop	1964
Mindbenders	A groovy kind of love	1966
Mindbenders	Ashes to ashes	1966
Mojos	Everything's alright	1964
Monkees	A little bit me, a little bit you	1967
Monkees	Alternate title	1967
Monkees	D.W.Washburn	1968
Monkees	Daydream believer	1967 1968
Monkees	I'm a believer	1967
Monkees	Pleasant Valley Sundays	1967
Monkees	Valleri	1968
Moody Blues	Go now	1965
Moody Blues	Nights in white satin	1968
Move	Blackberry Way	1969
Move	Fire Brigade	1968
Move	Flowers in the rain	1967
Move	I can hear the grass grow	1967
Move	Night of fear	1967
Move	Curly	1969
Mr Acker Bilk & His Paramount Jazz Band	Buona Sera	1961
Mr Acker Bilk & His Paramount Jazz Band	That's my home	1961
Mr. Acker Bilk & His Paramount Jazz Band	A taste of honey	1963
Mr. Acker Bilk & His Paramount Jazz Band	Lonely	1962
Mr. Acker Bilk & His Paramount Jazz Band	Stranger on the shore	1961 1962

Mr. Acker Bilk & His Paramount Jazz Band	Summer set	1960
Mrs. Mills	Mrs. Mills medley	1962
Nancy Sinatra	How does that grab you darlin'	1966
Nancy Sinatra	Sugar town	1967
Nancy Sinatra	These boots are made for walkin'	1966
Nancy Sinatra & Frank Sinatra	Somethin' stupid	1967
Nancy Sinatra / Nancy Sinatra & Lee Hazlewood	Jackson	1967
Nancy Sinatra / Nancy Sinatra & Lee Hazlewood	You only live twice	1967
Napoleon XIV	They're coming to take me away, ha ha!	1966
Nashville Teens	Google eye	1964
Nashville Teens	Tobacco Road	1964
Nat 'King' Cole	Just as much as ever	1960
Nat 'King' Cole	Ramblin' Rose	1962
Nat 'King' Cole	That's you	1960
Nat 'King' Cole & The George Shearing Quartet	Let there be love	1962
Ned Miller	From a Jack to a King	1963
Neil Christian	That's nice	1966
Neil Sedaka	Breaking up is hard to do	1962
Neil Sedaka	Calender girl	1961
Neil Sedaka	Happy birthday, sweet sixteen	1962
Neil Sedaka	Little devil	1961
Neil Sedaka	Oh Carol	1960
Neil Sedaka	Stairway to heaven	1960
New Vaudeville Band	Finchley central	1967
New Vaudeville Band	Peek-a-boo	1967
New Vaudeville Band	Winchester Cathedral	1966
Newbeats	Bread and butter	1964
Nina & Frederick	Little donkey	1960 1961
Nina Simone	Ain't got no - I got life	1968 1969
Nina Simone	Do what you gotta do	1968 1969
Nina Simone	To love somebody	1969
Nino Rosso	Il silenzio	1965

Artist	Title	Year
Nino Tempo & April Stevens	Deep purple	1963
Nino Tempo & April Stevens	Whispering	1964
Noel Harrison	The windmills of your mind	1969
O.C.Smith	The son of Hickory Holler's tramp	1968
Ohio Express	Yummy yummy yummy	1968
Oliver	Good morning starshine	1969
Otis Redding	(Sittin' on) the dock of the bay	1968
Otis Redding	Hard to handle	1968
Otis Redding	My girl	1966
Otis Redding & Carla Thomas	Tramp	1967
Overlanders	Michelle	1966
P.J.Proby	Hold me	1964
P.J.Proby	I apologize	1965
P.J.Proby	Let the water run down	1965
P.J.Proby	Maria	1965 1966
P.J.Proby	Somewhere	1964 1965
P.J.Proby	Together	1964
P.P.Arnold	The first cut is the deepest	1967
Paper Dolls	Something here in my heart	1968
Pat Boone	Johnny will	1961 1962
Pat Boone	Moody river	1961
Pat Boone	Speedy Gonzales	1962
Pat Boone	The main attraction	1962 1963
Paul & Barry Ryan	Don't bring me your heartaches	1965
Paul & Barry Ryan	Have pity on the boy	1966
Paul & Barry Ryan	I love her	1966
Paul & Paula	Hey Paula	1963
Paul & Paula	Young lovers	1963
Paul Anka	Love me warm and tender	1962
Paul Anka	Put your head on my shoulder	1960
Paul Jones	High time	1966
Paul Jones	I've been a bad bad boy	1967
Paul Mauriat	Love is blue (L'amour est bleu)	1968
Peddlers	Birth	1969

Percy Faith	Theme from 'A Summer Place'	1960
Percy Sledge	When a man loves a woman	1966
Perry Como	Delaware	1960
Peter & Gordon	A world without love	1964
Peter & Gordon	Baby I'm yours	1965
Peter & Gordon	Lady Godiva	1966
Peter & Gordon	Nobody I know	1964
Peter & Gordon	To know you is to love you	1965
Peter & Gordon	True love ways	1965
Peter Cook & Dudley Moore	Goodbye-ee	1965
Peter Sarstedt	Frozen orange juice	1969
Peter Sarstedt	Where do you go to (my lovely)	1969
Peter Sellers	A hard day's night	1966
Peter Sellers & Sophia Loren	Goodness gracious me	1960 1961
Peter, Paul & Mary	Blowing in the wind	1963
Petula Clark	Don't sleep in the subway	1967
Petula Clark	Downtown	1964 1965
Petula Clark	I couldn't live without your love	1966
Petula Clark	I know a place	1965
Petula Clark	My friend the sea	1961 1962
Petula Clark	My love	1966
Petula Clark	Romeo	1961
Petula Clark	Sailor	1961
Petula Clark	The other man's grass (is always greener)	1968
Petula Clark	This is my song	1967
Petula Clark	Ya Ya twist	1962
Pigmeat Markham	Here comes the judge	1968
Piltdown Men	Goodnight Mrs.Flintstone	1961
Piltdown Men	MacDonald's cave	1960
Piltdown Men	Piltdown rides again	1961
Pink Floyd	Arnold Layne	1967
Pink Floyd	See Emily play	1967
Pinkerton's Assorted Colours	Mirror, mirror	1966
Plastic Penny	Everything I am	1968
Platters	Harbour lights	1960

Artist	Song	Year
Pretty Things	Don't bring me down	1964
Pretty Things	Honey I need	1965
Prince Buster	Al Capone	1967
Procol Harum	A whiter shade of pale	1967
Procol Harum	Homburg	1967
R.Dean Taylor	Gotta see Jane	1968
Radha Krishna Temple	Hare Krishna mantra	1969
Ramrods	Riders in the sky	1961
Ray Charles	Hit the road Jack	1961
Ray Charles	I can't stop loving you	1962
Ray Charles	Take these chains from my heart	1963
Ray Charles	You don't know me	1962
Ray Charles	Your cheating heart	1963
Reparata & The Delrons	Captain of your ship	1968
Richard Anthony	If I loved you	1964
Richard Chamberlain	Hi-lili, hi-lo	1963
Richard Chamberlain	Love me tender	1962
Richard Chamberlain	Theme from 'Dr.Kildare' (Three stars will shine tonight)	1962
Richard Harris	MacArthur Park	1968
Ricky Nelson	Fools rush in	1963
Ricky Nelson	For you	1964
Ricky Nelson	Hello Mary Lou	1961
Ricky Nelson	Travellin' Man	1961
Ricky Nelson	Young world	1962
Ricky Valance	Tell Laura I love her	1960
Righteous Brothers	(You're my) soul and inspiration	1966
Righteous Brothers	Unchained melody	1965
Righteous Brothers	You've lost that lovin' feelin'	1965 1969
Robin Gibb	Saved by the bell	1969
Rockin' Berries	He's in town	1964
Rockin' Berries	Poor man's son	1965
Roger Miller	England swings	1966
Roger Miller	King of the road	1965
Roger Miller	Little green apples	1968
Roger Whittaker	Durham Town (the leavin')	1969
Rolf Harris	Sun arise	1962 1963
Rolf Harris	Tie me kangaroo down	1960
Rolf Harris	Two little boys	1969

Artist	Song	Year
Rolling Stones	(I can't get no) satisfaction	1965
Rolling Stones	19th nervous breakdown	1966
Rolling Stones	Dandelion	1967
Rolling Stones	Get off of my cloud	1965
Rolling Stones	Have you seen you mother, baby, standing in the shadow ?	1966
Rolling Stones	Honky Tonk women	1969
Rolling Stones	I wanna be your man	1963 1964
Rolling Stones	It's all over now	1964
Rolling Stones	Jumping Jack Flash	1968
Rolling Stones	Let's spend the night together	1967
Rolling Stones	Little red rooster	1964 1965
Rolling Stones	Not fade away	1964
Rolling Stones	Paint it black	1966
Rolling Stones	The last time	1965
Rolling Stones	We love you	1967
Ronettes	Baby, I love you	1964
Ronettes	Be my baby	1963
Ronnie Carroll	Roses are red (my love)	1962
Ronnie Carroll	Say wonderful things	1963
Rooftop Singers	Walk right in	1963
Roy 'C'	Shotgun wedding	1966
Roy Orbison	Blue angel	1960 1961
Roy Orbison	Blue Bayou	1963
Roy Orbison	Borne on the wind	1964
Roy Orbison	Crawlin' back	1965
Roy Orbison	Dream baby	1962
Roy Orbison	Falling	1963
Roy Orbison	Goodnight	1965
Roy Orbison	In dreams	1963
Roy Orbison	It's over	1964
Roy Orbison	Lana	1966
Roy Orbison	Mean woman blues	1963
Roy Orbison	Oh pretty woman	1964
Roy Orbison	Only the lonely	1960
Roy Orbison	Pretty paper	1964 1965
Roy Orbison	Runnin' scared	1961

Artist	Title	Year
Roy Orbison	There won't be many coming home	1966 1967
Roy Orbison	Too soon to know	1966
Royal Guardsmen	Snoopy vs The Red Baron	1967
Russ Conway	Lucky five	1960
Russ Conway	More and more party pops	1960
Russ Conway	Passing breeze	1960
Russ Conway	Pepe	1961
Russ Conway	Royal event	1960
Russ Conway	Snow coach	1960
Russ Conway	Toy balloons	1961 1962
Sam & Dave	Soul sister, brown sugar	1969
Sam Cooke	Chain gang	1960
Sam Cooke	Cupid	1961
Sam Cooke	Twistin' the night away	1962
Sam The Sham & The Pharoahs	Wooly bully	1965
Sandie Shaw	(There's) always something there to remind me	1964
Sandie Shaw	Girl don't come	1964 1965
Sandie Shaw	I'll stop at nothing	1965
Sandie Shaw	Long live love	1965
Sandie Shaw	Message understood	1965
Sandie Shaw	Monsieur Dupont	1969
Sandie Shaw	Nothing come easy	1966
Sandie Shaw	Puppet on a string	1967
Sandie Shaw	Tomorrow	1966
Sandie Shaw	You've not changed	1967
Sandpipers	Guantanamera	1966
Sandy Nelson	Let there be drums	1961 1962
Sandy Nelson	Teen beat	1960
Sandy Posey	Single girl	1967
Sarah Vaughan & Billy Eckstine	Passing strangers	1969
Scaffold	Lily the pink	1968 1969
Scaffold	Thank u very much	1967 1968

Artist	Song	Year
Scott McKenzie	San Francisco (Be sure to wear some flowers in your hair)	1967
Scott Walker	Joanna	1968
Scott Walker	Lights of Cincinnati	1969
Searchers	Don't throw your love away	1964
Searchers	Goodbye my love	1965
Searchers	He's got no love	1965
Searchers	Needles and pins	1964
Searchers	Some day we're gonna love again	1964
Searchers	Sugar and spice	1963
Searchers	Sweets for my sweet	1963
Searchers	Take me for what I'm worth	1966
Searchers	What have they done to the rain?	1964 1965
Searchers	When you walk in the room	1964
Seekers	A world of our own	1965
Seekers	Georgie girl	1967
Seekers	I'll never find another you	1965
Seekers	Morningtown ride	1966 1967
Seekers	Someday one day	1966
Seekers	The carnival is over	1965 1966
Seekers	Walk with me	1966
Seekers	When will the good apples fall	1967
Shadows	Apache	1960
Shadows	Atlantis	1963
Shadows	Dance on!	1962 1963
Shadows	Don't make my baby blue	1965
Shadows	F.B.I.	1961
Shadows	Foot tapper	1963
Shadows	Genie with the light brown lamp	1965
Shadows	Geronimo	1963 1964
Shadows	Guitar tango	1962
Shadows	Kon-Tiki	1961
Shadows	Man of mystery	1960 1961
Shadows	Mary Anne	1965

Shadows	Shindig	1963
Shadows	Stingray	1965
Shadows	The frightened city	1961
Shadows	The rise and fall of Flingel Bunt	1964
Shadows	The savage	1961 1962
Shadows	The stranger	1960 1961
Shadows	Theme for young lovers	1964
Shadows	War Lord	1965 1966
Shadows	Wonderful land	1962
Shane Fenton & The Fentones	Cindy's birthday	1962
Shangri-La's	Leader of the pack	1965
Shangri-La's	Remember (walkin' in the sand)	1964
Shirelles	Will you still love me tomorrow?	1961
Shirley Bassey	As long as he needs me	1960 1961
Shirley Bassey	Climb ev'ry mountain	1961
Shirley Bassey	I (who have nothing)	1963
Shirley Bassey	I'll get by	1962
Shirley Bassey	I'll get by (as long as I have you)	1961
Shirley Bassey	Reach for the stars	1961
Shirley Bassey	What now my love?	1962
Shirley Bassey	You'll never know	1961
Shirley Ellis	The clapping song	1965
Showstoppers	Ain't nothin' but a house party	1968
Simon & Garfunkel	April come she will)	1969
Simon & Garfunkel	Homeward bound	1966
Simon & Garfunkel	I am a rock	1966
Simon & Garfunkel	Mrs.Robinson	1968 1969
Simon & Garfunkel	The boxer	1969
Simon Dupree & The Big Sound	Kites	1967 1968
Singing Nun	Dominique	1963 1964
Sir Douglas Quintet	She's about a mover	1965
Skeeter Davis	The end of the world	1963
Sly & The Family Stone	Dance to the music	1968

Artist	Title	Year
Small Faces	All or nothing	1966
Small Faces	Here come the nice	1967
Small Faces	Hey girl	1966
Small Faces	Itchycoo Park	1967
Small Faces	Lazy Sunday	1968
Small Faces	My mind's eye	1966 1967
Small Faces	Sha la la la lee	1966
Small Faces	Tin soldier	1967 1968
Small Faces	Universal	1968
Small Faces	Whatcha gonna do about it	1965
Smokey Robinson & The Miracles	The tracks of my tears	1969
Solomon King	She wears my ring	1968
Sonny	Laugh at me	1965
Sonny & Cher	Baby don't go	1965
Sonny & Cher	But you're mine	1965
Sonny & Cher	I got you babe	1965
Sonny & Cher	Little man	1966
Sonny & Cher	What now my love	1966
Sounds Nice feat. Tim Mycroft	Love at first sight (Je t'aime….moi non plus)	1969
Sounds Orchestral	Cast your fate to the wind	1965
Spencer Davis Group	Gimme some loving	1966
Spencer Davis Group	I'm a man	1967
Spencer Davis Group	Keep on running	1965 1966
Spencer Davis Group	Somebody help me	1966
Spencer Davis Group	When I come home	1966
Spotnicks	Hava Nagila	1963
Springfields	Bambino	1961
Springfields	Island of dreams	1963
Springfields	Say I won't be there	1963
St.Louis Union	Girl	1966
Stan Getz & Charlie Byrd	Desafinado	1962 1963
Status Quo	Ice in the sun	1968
Status Quo	Pictures of matchstick men	1968
Steve Lawrence	Footsteps	1960

Artist	Song	Year
Steve Lawrence & Eydie Gorme	I want to stay here	1963
Stevie Wonder	A place in the sun	1967
Stevie Wonder	For once in my life	1969
Stevie Wonder	I don't know why I love you	1969
Stevie Wonder	I was made to love her	1967
Stevie Wonder	My cherie amour	1969
Stevie Wonder	Uptight (everything's alright)	1966
Stevie Wonder	Yester-me, yester-you, yesterday	1969
String-a-longs	Wheels	1961
Sue Nicholls	Where will you be?	1968
Supremes	Baby love	1964 1965
Supremes	Love is here and now you're gone	1967
Supremes	Stop! In the name of love	1965
Supremes	The happening	1967
Supremes	Where did our love go?	1964
Supremes	You can't hurry love	1966
Supremes	You keep me hangin' on	1966 1967
Surfaris	Wipe out	1963
Susan Maughan	Bobby's girl	1962 1963
Swinging Blue Jeans	Good golly Miss Molly	1964
Swinging Blue Jeans	Hippy hippy shake	1964
Swinging Blue Jeans	You're no good	1964
Temperance Seven	Pasadena	1961
Temperance Seven	You're driving me crazy	1961
Temptations	(I know) I'm losing you	1967
Temptations	Beauty is only skin deep	1966
Temptations	Cloud nine	1969
Temptations	Get ready	1969
Them	Baby please don't go	1965
Them	Here comes the night	1965
Thunderclap Newman	Something in the air	1969
Tokens	The lion sleeps tonight (Wimoweh)	1962
Tom Jones	A minute of your time	1968 1969
Tom Jones	Delilah	1968

Tom Jones	Detroit City	1967
Tom Jones	Funny familiar forgotten feelings	1967
Tom Jones	Green green grass of home	1966 1967
Tom Jones	Help yourself	1968
Tom Jones	I'll never fall in love again	1967
Tom Jones	I'm coming home	1967 1968
Tom Jones	It's not unusual	1965
Tom Jones	Love me tonight	1969
Tom Jones	Not responsible	1966
Tom Jones	Once there was a time	1966
Tom Jones	What's new pussycat?	1965
Tom Jones	With these hands	1965
Tom Jones	Without love	1969
Tommy Bruce & The Bruisers	Ain't misbehavin'	1960
Tommy James & The Shondells	Mony Mony	1968
Tommy Roe	Dizzy	1969
Tommy Roe	Everybody	1963
Tommy Roe	Sheila	1962
Tommy Roe	The folk singer	1963
Tommy Steele	Little white bull	1960
Tommy Steele	What a mouth	1960
Tony Orlando	Bless you	1961
Topol	If I were a rich man	1967
Tornados	Globetrotter	1963
Tornados	Robot	1963
Tornados	Telstar	1962 1963
Tornados	The Ice Cream man	1963
Toys	A lovers concerto	1965 1966
Traffic	Here we go round the Mulberry bush	1967 1968
Traffic	Hole in my shoe	1967
Traffic	Paper sun	1967
Tremeloes	(Call me) number one	1969
Tremeloes	Even the bad times are good	1967
Tremeloes	Hello world	1969

Artist	Title	Year
Tremeloes	Helule Helule	1968
Tremeloes	Here comes my baby	1967
Tremeloes	My little lady	1968
Tremeloes	Silence is golden	1967
Tremeloes	Suddenly you love me	1968
Trini Lopez	If I had a hammer	1963
Troggs	Anyway that you want me	1967
Troggs	Give it to me	1967
Troggs	I can't control myself	1966
Troggs	Love is all around	1967
Troggs	Night of the long grass	1967
Troggs	Wild thing	1966
Troggs	With a girl like you	1966
Turtles	Elenore	1968
Turtles	Happy together	1967
Turtles	She'd rather be with me	1967
Twinkle	Terry	1964 1965
Tymes	People	1969
Unit Four Plus Two	(You've) never been in love like this before	1965
Unit Four Plus Two	Concrete and clay	1965
Upsetters	Dollar in the teeth	1969
Upsetters	Return of Django	1969
Val Doonican	Elusive butterfly	1966
Val Doonican	If I knew then what I know now	1968
Val Doonican	If the whole world stopped loving	1967 1968
Val Doonican	Memories are made of this	1967
Val Doonican	The special years	1965
Val Doonican	Walk tall	1964 1965
Val Doonican	What would I be?	1966 1967
Vanilla Fudge	You keep me hanging on	1967
Vanity Fare	Early in the morning	1969
Vanity Fare	I live for the sun	1968
Ventures	Perfidia	1960 1961
Ventures	Walk don't run	1960
Vernons Girls	Lover please	1962

Artist	Title	Year
Vernons Girls	You know what I mean	1962
Vikki Carr	It must be him	1967
Vince Hill	Edelweiss	1967
Vince Hill	Roses of Picardy	1967
Vince Hill	Take me to your heart again	1966
Viscounts	Shortnin' bread	1960
Walker Brothers	(Baby) you don't have to tell me	1966
Walker Brothers	Another tear falls	1966
Walker Brothers	Love her	1965
Walker Brothers	Make it easy on yourself	1965
Walker Brothers	My ship is coming in	1965 1966
Walker Brothers	The sun ain't gonna shine anymore	1966
Wayne Fontana	Come on home	1966
Wayne Fontana	Pamela, Pamela	1967
Wayne Fontana & The Mindbenders	Just a little bit too late	1965
Wayne Fontana & The Mindbenders	The game of love	1965
Wayne Fontana & The Mindbenders	Um, um, um, um, um, um	1964
Whistling Jack Smith	I was Kaiser Bill's batman	1967
Who	Anyway, anyhow, anywhere	1965
Who	Happy Jack	1966 1967
Who	I can see for miles	1967
Who	I can't explain	1965
Who	I'm a boy	1966
Who	My generation	1965 1966
Who	Pictures of Lily	1967
Who	Pinball wizard	1969
Who	Substitute	1966
Wilson Pickett	Hey Jude	1969
Wilson Pickett	In the midnight hour	1965
Winifred Atwell	Piano party	1960
Wink Martindale	Deck of cards	1963
Yardbirds	Evil hearted you	1965
Yardbirds	For your love	1965
Yardbirds	Heart full of soul	1965

Yardbirds	Over under sideways down	1966
Yardbirds	Shapes of things	1966
Yardbirds	Still I'm sad	1965
Young Idea	With a little help from my friends	1967
Young Rascals	Groovin'	1967
Zager & Evans	In the year 2525 (Exordium and Terminus)	1969
Zombies	She's not there	1964

Alphabetical listing by title

Title	Artist	Year
(Baby) you don't have to tell me	Walker Brothers	1966
(Call me) number one	Tremeloes	1969
(I can't get no) satisfaction	Rolling Stones	1965
(I don't know why I love you) but I do	Clarence 'Frogman' Henry	1961
(I know) I'm losing you	Temptations	1967
(If paradise is) half as nice	Amen Corner	1969
(Marie's the name of) His latest flame	Elvis Presley	1961 1962
(Sittin' on) the dock of the bay	Otis Redding	1968
(There's) always something there to remind me	Sandie Shaw	1964
(Your love keeps lifting me) higher and higher	Jackie Wilson	1969
(You're my) soul and inspiration	Righteous Brothers	1966
(You're the) devil in disguise	Elvis Presley	1963
(You've) never been in love like this before	Unit Four Plus Two	1965
007 (Shanty town)	Desmond Dekker & The Aces	1967
1,2,3	Len Barry	1965 1966
1-2-3 O'Leary	Des O'Connor	1968 1969
19th nervous breakdown	Rolling Stones	1966
5-4-3-2-1	Manfred Mann	1964
76 Trombones	King Brothers	1961
A bad night	Cat Stevens	1967
A boy named Sue	Johnny Cash	1969
A day without love	Love Affair	1968
A fool am I	Cilla Black	1966
A forever kind of love	Bobby Vee	1962 1963
A girl like you	Cliff Richard	1961
A groovy kind of love	Mindbenders	1966
A hard day's night	Beatles	1964
A hard day's night	Peter Sellers	1966

A hundred pounds of clay	Craig Douglas	1961
A little bit me, a little bit you	Monkees	1967
A little bitty tear	Burl Ives	1962
A little bitty tear	Miki & Griff	1962
A little love, a little kiss	Karl Denver	1962
A little loving	Fourmost	1964
A love like yours	Ike & Tina Turner	1966
A lovers concerto	Toys	1965 1966
A man without love	Englebert Humperdinck	1968
A mess of blues	Elvis Presley	1960
A message to Martha (Kentucky Bluebird)	Adam Faith	1964 1965
A minute of your time	Tom Jones	1968 1969
A must to avoid	Herman's Hermits	1966
A picture of you	Joe Brown	1962
A place in the sun	Stevie Wonder	1967
A Scottish soldier (green hills of Tyrol)	Andy Stewart	1961
A taste of honey	Mr. Acker Bilk & His Paramount Jazz Band	1963
A thousand stars	Billy Fury	1961
A voice in the wilderness	Cliff Richard & The Shadows	1960
A whiter shade of pale	Procol Harum	1967
A world of our own	Seekers	1965
A world without love	Peter & Gordon	1964
African waltz	Johnny Dankworth	1961
Ain't gonna wash for a week	Brook Brothers	1961
Ain't got no - I got life	Nina Simone	1968 1969
Ain't misbehavin'	Tommy Bruce & The Bruisers	1960
Ain't nothin' but a house party	Showstoppers	1968
Ain't that funny	Jimmy Justice	1962
Ain't that lovin' you baby	Elvis Presley	1964
Al Capone	Prince Buster	1967
Albatross	Fleetwood Mac	1968 1969
Alfie	Cilla Black	1966
All alone am I	Brenda Lee	1963
All along the watchtower	Jimi Hendrix Experience	1968

All day and all of the night	Kinks	1964 1965
All I have to do is dream	Bobbie Gentry & Glen Campbell	1969
All I really want to do	Byrds	1965
All I really want to do	Cher	1965
All I see is you	Dusty Springfield	1966
All I want for Christmas is a Beatle	Dora Bryan	1964
All my love	Cliff Richard	1967 1968
All or nothing	Small Faces	1966
All over the world	Francoise Hardy	1965
All that I am	Elvis Presley	1966
All you need is love	Beatles	1967
Almost there	Andy Williams	1965
Alternate title	Monkees	1967
Am I that easy to forget?	Englebert Humperdinck	1968
Among my souvenirs	Connie Francis	1960
And the heaven's cried	Anthony Newley	1961
Angela Jones	Michael Cox	1960
Another tear falls	Walker Brothers	1966
Anyone who had a heart	Cilla Black	1964
Anyway that you want me	Troggs	1967
Anyway, anyhow, anywhere	Who	1965
Apache	Shadows	1960
Applejack	Jet Harris & Tony Meehan	1963
April come she will)	Simon & Garfunkel	1969
Aquarius / Let the sun shine in	5th Dimension	1969
Are you lonesome tonight?	Elvis Presley	1961
Are you sure ?	Allisons	1961
Arnold Layne	Pink Floyd	1967
As long as he needs me	Shirley Bassey	1960 1961
As tears go by	Marianne Faithfull	1964
As usual	Brenda Lee	1964
As you like it	Adam Faith	1962
Ashes to ashes	Mindbenders	1966
Atlantis	Shadows	1963
Autumn Almanac	Kinks	1967
Baby come back	Equals	1968

Baby don't go	Sonny & Cher	1965
Baby I don't care	Buddy Holly	1961
Baby I'm yours	Peter & Gordon	1965
Baby love	Supremes	1964 1965
Baby make it soon	Marmalade	1969
Baby now that I've found you	Foundations	1967
Baby please don't go	Them	1965
Baby Roo	Connie Francis	1961
Baby sittin' boogie	Buzz Clifford	1961
Baby, I love you	Ronettes	1964
Bachelor boy	Cliff Richard	1962 1963
Back on my feet again	Foundations	1968
Backstage	Gene Pitney	1966
Bad boy	Marty Wilde	1960
Bad moon rising	Creedence Clearwater Revival	1969
Bad to me	Billy J.Kramer & The Dakotas	1963
Badge	Cream	1969
Ballad of Paladin	Duane Eddy	1962
Bama lama bama loo	Little Richard	1964
Bambino	Springfields	1961
Bang bang (my baby shot me down)	Cher	1966
Barbara Ann	Beach Boys	1966
Be mine	Lance Fortune	1960
Be my baby	Ronettes	1963
Be my guest	Fats Domino	1960
Beatnik fly	Johnny & The Hurricanes	1960
Beauty is only skin deep	Temptations	1966
Because I love you	Georgie Fame	1967
Because of love	Billy Fury	1962
Because they're young	Duane Eddy	1960
Bee bom	Anthony Newley	1961
Behind a painted smile	Isley Brothers	1969
Bend it!	Dave Dee, Dozy, Beaky Mick & Tich	1966
Bend me, shape me	Amen Corner	1968
Bernadette	Four Tops	1967

Big bad John	Jimmy Dean	1961
		1962
Big girls don't cry	Four Seasons	1963
Big ship	Cliff Richard	1969
Birth	Peddlers	1969
Bits and pieces	Dave Clark Five	1964
Black girl	Four Pennies	1964
Black is black	Los Bravos	1966
Black velvet band	Dubliners	1967
Blackberry Way	Move	1969
Bless you	Tony Orlando	1961
Blowing in the wind	Peter, Paul & Mary	1963
Blue angel	Roy Orbison	1960
		1961
Blue Bayou	Roy Orbison	1963
Blue Christmas	Elvis Presley	1964
		1965
Blue eyes	Don Partridge	1968
Blue moon	Marcels	1961
Blue turns to grey	Cliff Richard	1966
Bo Diddley	Buddy Holly	1963
Bobby's girl	Susan Maughan	1962
		1963
Bongo blues	Cliff Richard & The Shadows	1960
Bonnie came back	Duane Eddy	1960
Boom bang-a-bang	Lulu	1969
Borne on the wind	Roy Orbison	1964
Bossa Nova baby	Elvis Presley	1963
Boy	Lulu	1968
Boys cry	Eden Kane	1964
Bread and butter	Newbeats	1964
Breakaway	Beach Boys	1969
Breakin' a brand new broken heart	Connie Francis	1961
Breakin' down the walls of heartache	Johnny Johnson & His Bandwagon	1968 1969
Breaking up is hard to do	Neil Sedaka	1962
Bring it on home to me	Animals	1965
Bringing on back the good times	Love Affair	1969
Brown-eyed handsome man	Buddy Holly	1963

Title	Artist	Year
Build me up buttercup	Foundations	1968 1969
Buona Sera	Mr Acker Bilk & His Paramount Jazz Band	1961
Burning of the midnight lamp	Jimi Hendrix Experience	1967
Bus stop	Hollies	1966
But you love me Daddy	Jim Reeves	1969
But you're mine	Sonny & Cher	1965
Cabaret	Louis Armstrong	1968
Calender girl	Neil Sedaka	1961
Call up the groups (medley)	Barron Knights	1964
Can you please crawl out your window?	Bob Dylan	1966
Candy man	Brian Poole & The Tremeloes	1964
Can't buy me love	Beatles	1964
Can't get used to losing you	Andy Williams	1963
Can't help falling in love	Elvis Presley	1962
Can't take my eyes off you	Andy Williams	1968
Can't you see that she's mine	Dave Clark Five	1964
Captain of your ship	Reparata & The Delrons	1968
Careless hands	Des O'Connor	1967 1968
Carrie-Anne	Hollies	1967
Cast your fate to the wind	Sounds Orchestral	1965
Catch the wind	Donovan	1965
Catch us if you can	Dave Clark Five	1965
Cathy's clown	Everly Brothers	1960
Chain gang	Sam Cooke	1960
Charmaine	Bachelors	1963
Cinderella Rockefella	Esther & Abi Ofarim	1968
Cindy's birthday	Shane Fenton & The Fentones	1962
Classical gas	Mason Williams	1968
Clementine	Bobby Darin	1960
Climb ev'ry mountain	Shirley Bassey	1961
Cloud nine	Temptations	1969
Cold turkey	John Lennon & Yoko One With The Plastic Ono Band	1969
Collette	Billy Fury	1960
Colours	Donovan	1965
Come and stay with me	Marianne Faithfull	1965

Come back and shake me	Clodagh Rodgers	1969
Come home	Dave Clark Five	1965
Come on home	Wayne Fontana	1966
Come outside	Mike Sarne & Wendy Richard	1962
Come together	Beatles	1969
Come tomorrow	Manfred Mann	1965
Coming home baby	Mel Torme	1963
Concrete and clay	Unit Four Plus Two	1965
Confessin' (that I love you)	Frank Ifield	1963
Congratulations	Cliff Richard	1968
Constantly	Cliff Richard	1964
Conversations	Cilla Black	1969
Counting teardrops	Emile Ford & The Checkmates	1960 1961
Country boy	Fats Domino	1960
Cradle of love	Johnny Preston	1960
Crawlin' back	Roy Orbison	1965
Creeque Alley	Mamas & Papas	1967
Cry like a baby	Box Tops	1968
Crying in the chapel	Elvis Presley	1965
Cupid	Johnny Nash	1969
Cupid	Sam Cooke	1961
Curly	Move	1969
D.W.Washburn	Monkees	1968
Da doo ron ron	Crystals	1963
Dance on!	Kathy Kirby	1963
Dance on!	Shadows	1962 1963
Dance to the music	Sly & The Family Stone	1968
Dance with me	Drifters	1960
Dance with the guitar man	Duane Eddy & The Rebelettes	1962 1963
Dancin' party	Chubby Checker	1962
Dancing in the street	Martha Reeves & The Vandellas	1969
Dandelion	Rolling Stones	1967
Darlin'	Beach Boys	1968
Day tripper	Beatles	1965 1966
Daydream	Lovin' Spoonful	1966

Daydream believer	Monkees	1967 1968
Days	Kinks	1968
Dead end street	Kinks	1966 1967
Death of a clown	Dave Davies	1967
Deck of cards	Wink Martindale	1963
Dedicated follower of fashion	Kinks	1966
Dedicated to the one I love	Mamas & Papas	1967
Deep in the heart of Texas	Duane Eddy	1962
Deep purple	Nino Tempo & April Stevens	1963
Delaware	Perry Como	1960
Delilah	Tom Jones	1968
Delta lady	Joe Cocker	1969
Desafinado	Stan Getz & Charlie Byrd	1962 1963
Detroit City	Tom Jones	1967
Devil woman	Marty Robbins	1962 1963
Diamonds	Jet Harris & Tony Meehan	1963
Diane	Bachelors	1964
Dick-a-dum-dum (King's Road)	Des O'Connor	1969
Distant drums	Jim Reeves	1966 1967
Dizzy	Tommy Roe	1969
Do it again	Beach Boys	1968
Do the clam	Elvis Presley	1965
Do wah diddy diddy	Manfred Mann	1964
Do what you gotta do	Nina Simone	1968 1969
Do what you gotta do	Four Tops	1969
Do you know the way to San Jose?	Dionne Warwick	1968
Do you love me?	Brian Poole & The Tremeloes	1963
Do you mind?	Anthony Newley	1960
Do you really love me too?	Billy Fury	1964
Do you want to dance	Cliff Richard	1962
Do you want to know a secret?	Billy J.Kramer & The Dakotas	1963
Dollar in the teeth	Upsetters	1969
Dominique	Singing Nun	1963 1964

Don't answer me	Cilla Black	1966
Don't blame me	Everly Brothers	1961
Don't blame me	Frank Ifield	1964
Don't bring Lulu	Dorothy Provine	1962
Don't bring me down	Animals	1966
Don't bring me down	Pretty Things	1964
Don't bring me your heartaches	Paul & Barry Ryan	1965
Don't ever change	Buddy Holly & The Crickets	1962
Don't forget to remember	Bee Gees	1969
Don't let me be misunderstood	Animals	1965
Don't let the sun catch you crying	Gerry & The Pacemakers	1964
Don't make my baby blue	Shadows	1965
Don't sleep in the subway	Petula Clark	1967
Don't stop the carnival	Alan Price Set	1968
Don't talk to him	Cliff Richard	1963 1964
Don't that beat all	Adam Faith	1962
Don't throw your love away	Searchers	1964
Don't treat me like a child	Helen Shapiro	1961
Don't turn around	Merseybeats	1964
Don't you know it ?	Adam Faith	1961
Don't you think it's time ?	Mike Berry & The Outlaws	1963
Down yonder	Johnny & The Hurricanes	1960
Downtown	Petula Clark	1964 1965
Dream a little dream of me	Mama Cass	1968
Dream baby	Roy Orbison	1962
Dreamin'	Johnny Burnette	1960 1961
Durham Town (the leavin')	Roger Whittaker	1969
Early in the morning	Vanity Fare	1969
Easily fall in love with you	Cliff Richard & The Shadows	1960
Easy going me	Adam Faith	1961
Ebony eyes	Everly Brothers	1961
Edelweiss	Vince Hill	1967
El Paso	Marty Robbins	1960
Eleanor Rigby	Beatles	1966
Elenore	Turtles	1968
Elouise	Barry Ryan	1968
Elusive butterfly	Bob Lind	1966

Elusive butterfly	Val Doonican	1966
England swings	Roger Miller	1966
English country garden	Jimmy Rodgers	1962
Eve of destruction	Barry McGuire	1965
Even the bad times are good	Tremeloes	1967
Everlasting love	Love Affair	1968
Everybody	Tommy Roe	1963
Everybody knows	Dave Clark Five	1967 1968
Everybody loves somebody sometime	Dean Martin	1964
Everybody's gonna be happy	Kinks	1965
Everybody's somebody's fool	Connie Francis	1960
Everyone's gone to the moon	Jonathan King	1965
Everything I am	Plastic Penny	1968
Everything's alright	Mojos	1964
Evil hearted you	Yardbirds	1965
Excerpt from 'A Teenage Opera'	Keith West	1967
F.B.I.	Shadows	1961
Falling	Roy Orbison	1963
Feel so fine	Johnny Preston	1960
Ferry 'cross the Mersey	Gerry & The Paceakers	1965
Finchley central	New Vaudeville Band	1967
Fings ain't wot they used to be	Max Bygraves	1960
Fire Brigade	Move	1968
Fire!	Crazy World Of Arthur Brown	1968
First of May	Bee Gees	1969
Five little fingers	Frankie McBride	1967
Flowers in the rain	Move	1967
Fools rush in	Ricky Nelson	1963
Foot tapper	Shadows	1963
Footsteps	Steve Lawrence	1960
For once in my life	Stevie Wonder	1969
For you	Ricky Nelson	1964
For your love	Yardbirds	1965
Forget him	Bobby Rydell	1963
Forget me not	Eden Kane	1962
Fox on the run	Manfred Mann	1969
Friday on my mind	Easybeats	1966 1967

From a Jack to a King	Ned Miller	1963
From a window	Billy J.Kramer & The Dakotas	1964
From me to you	Beatles	1963
From Russia with love	Matt Monro	1963
From the underworld	Herd	1967
Frozen orange juice	Peter Sarstedt	1969
Funny familiar forgotten feelings	Tom Jones	1967
Funny how love can be	Ivy League	1965
Galveston	Glen Campbell	1969
Games people play	Joe South	1969
Gather in the mushrooms	Benny Hill	1961
Gee whizz it's you	Cliff Richard	1961
Genie with the light brown lamp	Shadows	1965
Gentle on my mind	Dean Martin	1969
Georgie girl	Seekers	1967
Geronimo	Shadows	1963 1964
Get back	Beatles & Billy Preston	1969
Get lost	Eden Kane	1961
Get off of my cloud	Rolling Stones	1965
Get ready	Temptations	1969
Getaway	Georgie Fame & The Blue Flames	1966
Gimme little sign	Brenton Wood	1968
Gimme some loving	Spencer Davis Group	1966
Gimme, gimme, good loving	Crazy Elephant	1969
Gin house blues	Amen Corner	1967
Ginny come lately	Brian Hyland	1962
Girl	St.Louis Union	1966
Girl don't come	Sandie Shaw	1964 1965
Give it to me	Troggs	1967
Give peace a chance	John Lennon & Yoko One With The Plastic Ono Band	1969
Glad all over	Dave Clark Five	1963 1964
Globetrotter	Tornados	1963
Go away little girl	Mark Wynter	1963
Go now	Moody Blues	1965
God only knows	Beach Boys	1966
Going back	Dusty Springfield	1966

Going up the country	Canned Heat	1969
Goo Goo Barabajagal (Love is hot)	Donovan & Jeff Beck Group	1969
Good golly Miss Molly	Swinging Blue Jeans	1964
Good luck charm	Elvis Presley	1962
Good morning starshine	Oliver	1969
Good old rock 'n' roll	Dave Clark Five	1969
Good times	Cliff Richard	1969
Good times	Eric Burdon & The Animals	1967
Good timin'	Jimmy Jones	1960
Good vibrations	Beach Boys	1966 1967
Goodbye	Mary Hopkin	1969
Goodbye my love	Searchers	1965
Goodbye-ee	Peter Cook & Dudley Moore	1965
Goodness gracious me	Peter Sellers & Sophia Loren	1960 1961
Goodnight	Roy Orbison	1965
Goodnight midnight	Clodagh Rodgers	1969
Goodnight Mrs.Flintstone	Piltdown Men	1961
Google eye	Nashville Teens	1964
Got to get you into my life	Cliff Bennett & The Rebel Rousers	1966
Gotta see Jane	R.Dean Taylor	1968
Granada	Frank Sinatra	1961
Green green grass of home	Tom Jones	1966 1967
Green river	Creedence Clearwater Revival	1969
Green tambourine	Lemon Pipers	1968
Groovin'	Young Rascals	1967
Guantanamera	Sandpipers	1966
Guitar man	Elvis Presley	1968
Guitar tango	Shadows	1962
Gurney Slade	Max Harris	1960 1961
Ha! Ha! Said the clown	Manfred Mann	1967
Halfway to Paradise	Billy Fury	1961
Handy man	Jimmy Jones	1960
Hang on Sloopy	McCoys	1965
Happy birthday, sweet sixteen	Neil Sedaka	1962

Happy heart	Andy Williams	1969
Happy Jack	Who	1966 1967
Happy together	Turtles	1967
Harbour lights	Platters	1960
Hard to handle	Otis Redding	1968
Hare Krishna mantra	Radha Krishna Temple	1969
Harlem shuffle	Bob & Earl	1969
Harper Valley P.T.A.	Jeannie C.Riley	1968
Harvest of love	Benny Hill	1963
Hats off to Larry	Del Shannon	1961
Hava Nagila	Spotnicks	1963
Have a drink on me	Lonnie Donegan	1961
Have I the right?	Honeycombs	1964
Have pity on the boy	Paul & Barry Ryan	1966
Have you seen you mother, baby, standing in the shadow ?	Rolling Stones	1966
He ain't heavy...he's my brother	Hollies	1969
Headline news	Edwin Starr	1969
Heart full of soul	Yardbirds	1965
Heartaches by the number	Guy Mitchell	1960
He'll have to go	Jim Reeves	1960
Hello goodbye	Beatles	1967 1968
Hello I love you	Doors	1968
Hello little girl	Fourmost	1963
Hello Mary Lou	Ricky Nelson	1961
Hello Muddah! Hello Fadduh!	Allan Sherman	1963
Hello Suzie	Amen Corner	1969
Hello world	Tremeloes	1969
Hello, Dolly!	Frankie Vaughan	1964
Hello, Dolly!	Louis Armstrong	1964
Hello, how are you ?	Easybeats	1968
Help me girl	Eric Burdon & The Animals	1966
Help yourself	Tom Jones	1968
Help!	Beatles	1965
Helule Helule	Tremeloes	1968
Here come the nice	Small Faces	1967
Here comes my baby	Tremeloes	1967
Here comes that feeling	Brenda Lee	1962
Here comes the judge	Pigmeat Markham	1968

Here comes the night	Them	1965
Here I go again	Hollies	1964
Here it comes again	Fortunes	1965
Here we go round the Mulberry bush	Traffic	1967 1968
Heroes and villains	Beach Boys	1967
He's a rebel	Crystals	1963
He's got no love	Searchers	1965
He's in town	Rockin' Berries	1964
He's so fine	Chiffons	1963
Hey girl	Small Faces	1966
Hey Joe	Jimi Hendrix Experience	1967
Hey Jude	Beatles	1968
Hey Jude	Wilson Pickett	1969
Hey Paula	Paul & Paula	1963
Hey! Baby	Bruce Chanel	1962
Hey! Little girl	Del Shannon	1962
Hi ho silver lining	Jeff Beck	1967
Hideaway	Dave Dee, Dozy, Beaky Mick & Tich	1966
High in the sky	Amen Corner	1968
High time	Paul Jones	1966
Hi-lili, hi-lo	Richard Chamberlain	1963
Hi-lili, hi-lo	Alan Price Set	1966
Hippy hippy shake	Swinging Blue Jeans	1964
Hit and miss	John Barry Seven	1960
Hit the road Jack	Ray Charles	1961
Hold me	P.J.Proby	1964
Hold me tight	Johnny Nash	1968
Hold tight!	Dave Dee, Dozy, Beaky Mick & Tich	1966
Hole in my shoe	Traffic	1967
Hole in the ground	Bernard Cribbins	1962
Holy cow	Lee Dorsey	1966 1967
Homburg	Procol Harum	1967
Homeward bound	Simon & Garfunkel	1966
Honey	Bobby Goldsboro	1968
Honey I need	Pretty Things	1965
Honky Tonk women	Rolling Stones	1969
House of the rising sun	Animals	1964

How about that!	Adam Faith	1960
How can I meet her	Everly Brothers	1962
How do you do it?	Gerry & The Pacemakers	1963
How does that grab you darlin'	Nancy Sinatra	1966
How many tears	Bobby Vee	1961
How soon	Henry Mancini & His Orchestra	1964
Hubble bubble (toil and trouble)	Manfred Mann	1964
Hungry for love	Johnny Kidd & The Pirates	1963
Hurdy Gurdy Man	Donovan	1968
Hush…not a word to Mary	John Rowles	1968
I (who have nothing)	Shirley Bassey	1963
I am a rock	Simon & Garfunkel	1966
I am the walrus	Beatles	1967 1968
I apologize	P.J.Proby	1965
I believe	Bachelors	1964
I can hear music	Beach Boys	1969
I can hear the grass grow	Move	1967
I can see for miles	Who	1967
I can sing a rainbow - love is blue (medley)	Dells	1969
I can take or leave your loving	Herman's Hermits	1968
I can't control myself	Troggs	1966
I can't explain	Who	1965
I can't let go	Hollies	1966
I can't let Maggie go	Honeybus	1968
I can't stop loving you	Ray Charles	1962
I close my eyes and count to ten	Dusty Springfield	1968
I could easily fall	Cliff Richard	1964 1965
I couldn't live without your love	Petula Clark	1966
I don't care	Los Bravos	1966
I don't know why	Eden Kane	1962
I don't know why I love you	Stevie Wonder	1969
I don't want our loving to die	Herd	1968
I feel fine	Beatles	1964 1965
I feel free	Cream	1967
I feel love coming on	Felice Taylor	1967
I feel so bad	Elvis Presley	1961

I found out the hard way	Four Pennies	1964
I get around	Beach Boys	1964
I got you babe	Sonny & Cher	1965
I guess I'll always love you	Isley Brothers	1969
I heard it through the grapevine	Marvin Gaye	1969
I just don't know what to do with myself	Dusty Springfield	1964
I know a place	Petula Clark	1965
I like it	Gerry & The Pacemakers	1963
I live for the sun	Vanity Fare	1968
I love her	Paul & Barry Ryan	1966
I love how you love me	Jimmy Crawford	1961
I love you	Cliff Richard	1960 1961
I love you baby	Freddie & The Dreamers	1964
I love you because	Jim Reeves	1964
I must be seeing things	Gene Pitney	1965
I only want to be with you	Dusty Springfield	1963 1964
I pretend	Des O'Connor	1968
I put a spell on you	Alan Price Set	1966
I remember you	Frank Ifield	1962
I saw her again	Mamas & Papas	1966
I say a little prayer	Aretha Franklin	1968
I second that emotion	Diana Ross & The Supremes & The Temptations	1969
I think of you	Merseybeats	1964
I understand	Freddie & The Dreamers	1964 1965
I understand (just how you feel)	G-Clefs	1961 1962
I wanna be your man	Rolling Stones	1963 1964
I wanna go home	Lonnie Donegan	1960
I want to hold your hand	Beatles	1963 1964
I want to stay here	Steve Lawrence & Eydie Gorme	1963
I want you	Bob Dylan	1966
I was Kaiser Bill's batman	Whistling Jack Smith	1967
I was made to love her	Stevie Wonder	1967

Title	Artist	Year
I will	Billy Fury	1964
I wonder	Brenda Lee	1963
I won't come in while he's there	Jim Reeves	1967
I won't forget you	Jim Reeves	1964
I wouldn't trade you for the world	Bachelors	1964
Ice in the sun	Status Quo	1968
I'd never find another you	Billy Fury	1962
I'd rather go blind	Chicken Shack	1969
If every day was like Christmas	Elvis Presley	1966 1967
If I can dream	Elvis Presley	1969
If I had a hammer	Trini Lopez	1963
If I knew then what I know now	Val Doonican	1968
If I loved you	Richard Anthony	1964
If I needed someone	Hollies	1966
If I only had time	John Rowles	1968
If I ruled the world	Harry Secombe	1963
If I were a carpenter	Bobby Darin	1966
If I were a carpenter	Four Tops	1968
If I were a rich man	Topol	1967
If she should come to you	Anthony Newley	1960
If the whole world stopped loving	Val Doonican	1967 1968
If you gotta go, go now	Manfred Mann	1965
If you gotta make a fool of somebody	Freddie & The Dreamers	1963
Il silenzio	Nino Rosso	1965
I'll be there	Gerry & The Pacemakers	1965
I'll do my crying in the rain	Everly Brothers	1962
I'll get by	Shirley Bassey	1962
I'll get by (as long as I have you)	Shirley Bassey	1961
I'll keep you satisfied	Billy J.Kramer & The Dakotas	1963 1964
I'll never fall in love again	Bobbie Gentry	1969
I'll never fall in love again	Tom Jones	1967
I'll never find another you	Seekers	1965
I'll never get over you	Johnny Kidd & The Pirates	1963
I'll pick a rose for my rose	Marv Johnson	1969
I'll stop at nothing	Sandie Shaw	1965
I'll try anything	Dusty Springfield	1967
I'm a believer	Monkees	1967

I'm a better man	Engelbert Humperdinck	1969
I'm a boy	Who	1966
I'm a man	Spencer Davis Group	1967
I'm a tiger	Lulu	1968 1969
I'm alive	Hollies	1965
I'm coming home	Tom Jones	1967 1968
I'm crying	Animals	1964
I'm gonna be strong	Gene Pitney	1964 1965
I'm gonna get me a gun	Cat Stevens	1967
I'm gonna make you love me	Diana Ross & The Supremes & The Temptations	1969
I'm gonna make you mine	Lou Christie	1969
I'm in love	Fourmost	1964
I'm into something good	Herman's Hermits	1964
I'm just a baby	Louise Cordet	1962
I'm living in shame	Diana Ross & The Supremes	1969
I'm looking out the window	Cliff Richard	1962
I'm lost without you	Billy Fury	1965
I'm sorry	Brenda Lee	1960
I'm tellin' you now	Freddie & The Dreamers	1963
I'm the lonely one	Cliff Richard	1964
I'm the one	Gerry & The Pacemakers	1964
I'm the urban spaceman	Bonzo Dog Doo-Dah Band	1968 1969
Image of a girl	Mark Wynter	1960
In and out of love	Diana Ross & The Supremes	1967 1968
In dreams	Roy Orbison	1963
In summer	Billy Fury	1963
In the bad, bad old days	Foundations	1969
In the country	Cliff Richard & The Shadows	1967
In the ghetto	Elvis Presley	1969
In the middle of nowhere	Dusty Springfield	1965
In the midnight hour	Wilson Pickett	1965
In the mood	Ernie Fields & His Orchestra	1960
In the year 2525 (Exordium and Terminus)	Zager & Evans	1969
In thoughts of you	Billy Fury	1965

Inside - looking out	Animals	1966
Is it really over	Jim Reeves	1965
Is it true?	Brenda Lee	1964
Island of dreams	Springfields	1963
It hurts so much (to see you go)	Jim Reeves	1965
It miek	Desmond Dekker & The Aces	1969
It might as well rain until September	Carole King	1962
It must be him	Vikki Carr	1967
It only took a minute	Joe Brown	1962 1963
It started all over again	Brenda Lee	1962
It takes two	Marvin Gaye & Kim Weston	1967
Itchycoo Park	Small Faces	1967
It'll be me	Cliff Richard	1962
It's a man's man's man's world	James Brown	1966
It's all in the game	Cliff Richard	1963
It's all over	Cliff Richard	1967
It's all over now	Rolling Stones	1964
It's almost tomorrow	Mark Wynter	1963
It's for you	Cilla Black	1964
It's getting better	Mama Cass	1969
It's good news week	Hedgehoppers Anonymous	1965
It's my life	Animals	1965
It's my party	Lesley Gore	1963
It's not unusual	Tom Jones	1965
It's now or never	Elvis Presley	1960 1961
It's only make believe	Billy Fury	1964
It's over	Roy Orbison	1964
Itsy bitsy teeny weeny yellow polka dot bikini	Brian Hyland	1960
I've been a bad bad boy	Paul Jones	1967
I've been wrong before	Cilla Black	1965
I've got you under my skin	Four Seasons	1966
I've gotta get a message to you	Bee Gees	1968
I've told every little star	Linda Scott	1961
Jackson	Nancy Sinatra / Nancy Sinatra & Lee Hazlewood	1967
Ja-da	Johnny & The Hurricanes	1961

Je t'aime....moi non plus	Jane Birkin & Serge Gainsbourg	1969
Jealousy	Billy Fury	1961
Jeannie	Danny Williams	1962
Jennifer Eccles	Hollies	1968
Jennifer Juniper	Donovan	1968
Jesamine	Casuals	1968
Jezebel	Marty Wilde	1962
Jingle bell rock	Max Bygraves	1960
Joanna	Scott Walker	1968
Johnny remember me	John Leyton	1961
Johnny will	Pat Boone	1961 1962
Judy in disguise (with glasses)	John Fred & The Playboy Band	1968
Juliet	Four Pennies	1964
Jumping Jack Flash	Rolling Stones	1968
Just a little bit better	Herman's Hermits	1965
Just a little bit too late	Wayne Fontana & The Mindbenders	1965
Just as much as ever	Nat 'King' Cole	1960
Just like a woman	Manfred Mann	1966
Just like Eddie	Heinz	1963
Just loving you	Anita Harris	1967
Just one look	Hollies	1964
Just one smile	Gene Pitney	1966 1967
Keep on	Bruce Chanel	1968
Keep on running	Spencer Davis Group	1965 1966
Keep searchin' (we'll follow the sun)	Del Shannon	1965
King Midas in reverse	Hollies	1967
King of the road	Roger Miller	1965
Kiss me quick	Elvis Presley	1964
Kissin' cousins	Elvis Presley	1964
Kites	Simon Dupree & The Big Sound	1967 1968
Knock on wood	Eddie Floyd	1967
Kommotion	Duane Eddy	1960
Kon-Tiki	Shadows	1961

Title	Artist	Year
La mer (Beyond the sea)	Bobby Darin	1960
Lady Godiva	Peter & Gordon	1966
Lady Madonna	Beatles	1968
Lady Willpower	Gary Puckett & The Union Gap	1968
Lana	Roy Orbison	1966
Last night in Soho	Dave Dee, Dozy, Beaky, Mick & Tich	1968
Last night was made for love	Billy Fury	1962
Laugh at me	Sonny	1965
Lay lady lay	Bob Dylan	1969
Lazy river	Bobby Darin	1961
Lazy Sunday	Small Faces	1968
Leader of the pack	Shangri-La's	1965
Leave a little love	Lulu	1965
Les bicyclettes de Belsize	Englebert Humperdinck	1968
Let it be me	Everly Brothers	1960
Let it rock	Chuck Berry	1963
Let me cry on your shoulder	Ken Dodd	1967
Let me go, lover	Kathy Kirby	1964
Let the heartaches begin	Long John Baldry	1967 1968
Let the little girl dance	Billy Bland	1960
Let the water run down	P.J.Proby	1965
Let there be drums	Sandy Nelson	1961 1962
Let there be love	Nat 'King' Cole & The George Shearing Quartet	1962
Let's dance	Chris Montez	1962 1963
Let's get together	Hayley Mills	1961
Let's go to San Francisco	Flower Pot Men	1967
Let's hang on	Four Seasons	1965 1966
Let's jump the broomstick	Brenda Lee	1961
Let's pretend	Lulu	1967
Let's spend the night together	Rolling Stones	1967
Let's think about livin'	Bob Luman	1960
Let's turkey trot	Little Eva	1963
Let's twist again	Chubby Checker	1962
Light my fire	Jose Feliciano	1968

Lightning strikes	Lou Christie	1966
Lights of Cincinnati	Scott Walker	1969
Like a baby	Len Barry	1966
Like a child	Julie Rogers	1965
Like a rolling stone	Bob Dylan	1965
Like dreamers do	Applejacks	1964
Like I do	Maureen Evans	1962 1963
Like I've never been gone	Billy Fury	1963
Like strangers	Everly Brothers	1961
Lily the pink	Scaffold	1968 1969
Listen to me	Hollies	1968
Little arrows	Leapy Lee	1968
Little boy sad	Johnny Burnette	1961
Little by little	Dusty Springfield	1966
Little children	Billy J.Kramer & The Dakotas	1964
Little devil	Neil Sedaka	1961
Little donkey	Beverley Sisters	1960
Little donkey	Nina & Frederick	1960 1961
Little girl	Marty Wilde	1961
Little green apples	Roger Miller	1968
Little man	Sonny & Cher	1966
Little Miss Lonely	Helen Shapiro	1962
Little red rooster	Rolling Stones	1964 1965
Little sister	Elvis Presley	1961 1962
Little things	Dave Berry	1965
Little town flirt	Del Shannon	1963
Little white bull	Tommy Steele	1960
Lively	Lonnie Donegan	1960 1961
Living in the past	Jethro Tull	1969
Loneliness	Des O'Connor	1969
Lonely	Mr. Acker Bilk & His Paramount Jazz Band	1962
Lonely city	John Leyton	1962
Lonely pup (in a Christmas shop)	Adam Faith	1960 1961

Title	Artist	Year
Lonesome	Adam Faith	1962
Long live love	Sandie Shaw	1965
Look for a star	Gary Mills	1960
Look through any window	Hollies	1965
Looking high, high, high	Bryan Johnson	1960
Looking through the eyes of love	Gene Pitney	1965
Loop-de-loop	Frankie Vaughan	1963
Lorelei	Lonnie Donegan	1960
Losing you	Brenda Lee	1963
Losing you	Dusty Springfield	1964
Love	Cliff Richard & The Shadows	1960
Love at first sight (Je t'aime....moi non plus)	Sounds Nice feat. Tim Mycroft	1969
Love child	Diana Ross & The Supremes	1968 1969
Love her	Walker Brothers	1965
Love is all	Malcolm Roberts	1969
Love is all around	Troggs	1967
Love is blue (L'amour est bleu)	Paul Mauriat	1968
Love is here and now you're gone	Supremes	1967
Love is like a violin	Ken Dodd	1960
Love is strange	Everly Brothers	1965
Love letters	Elvis Presley	1966
Love letters	Ketty Lester	1962
Love me do	Beatles	1962 1963
Love me tender	Richard Chamberlain	1962
Love me tonight	Tom Jones	1969
Love me warm and tender	Paul Anka	1962
Lover please	Vernons Girls	1962
Lovers of the world unite	David & Jonathan	1966
Love's been good to me	Frank Sinatra	1969
Love's just a broken heart	Cilla Black	1966
Lovesick blues	Frank Ifield	1962 1963
Lovin' things	Marmalade	1968
Lucille	Everly Brothers	1960
Lucky five	Russ Conway	1960
Lucky lips	Cliff Richard	1963
Lumbered	Lonnie Donegan	1961
MacArthur Park	Richard Harris	1968

MacDonald's cave	Piltdown Men	1960
Mack the Knife	Bobby Darin	1960
Mack the Knife	Ella Fitzgerald	1960
Made you	Adam Faith	1960
Magical mystery tour	Beatles	1967 1968
Mais oui	King Brothers	1960
Make it easy on yourself	Walker Brothers	1965
Make me an island	Joe Dolan	1969
Make the world go away	Eddy Arnold	1966
Mama	Connie Francis	1960
Mama	Dave Berry	1966
Man of mystery	Shadows	1960 1961
Man of the world	Fleetwood Mac	1969
Many tears ago	Connie Francis	1961
March of the Siamese children	Kenny Ball & His Jazzmen	1962
Marcheta	Karl Denver	1961
Maria	P.J.Proby	1965 1966
Maria Elena	Los Indios Tagajaras	1963 1964
Marie	Bachelors	1965
Marrakesh Express	Crosby, Still & Nash	1969
Marry me	Mike Preston	1961
Marta	Bachelors	1967
Mary Anne	Shadows	1965
Massachusetts	Bee Gees	1967
Matthew and son	Cat Stevens	1967
May each day	Andy Williams	1966
May I have the next dream with you?	Malcolm Roberts	1968 1969
Maybe I know	Lesley Gore	1964
Me and my shadow	Frank Sinatra & Sammy Davis Jr.	1963
Me, the peaceful heart	Lulu	1968
Mean woman blues	Roy Orbison	1963
Mellow yellow	Donovan	1967
Melting pot	Blue Mink	1969
Memories are made of this	Val Doonican	1967
Memphis Tennessee	Chuck Berry	1963

Title	Artist	Year
Memphis Tennessee	Dave Berry & The Cruisers	1963
Merry gentle pops	Barron Knights	1965 1966
Message understood	Sandie Shaw	1965
Mexicali Rose	Karl Denver	1961
Mexico	Long John Baldry	1968
Michael	Highwaymen	1961
Michael, row the boat	Lonnie Donegan	1961
Michelle	David & Jonathan	1966
Michelle	Overlanders	1966
Midnight in Moscow	Kenny Ball & His Jazzmen	1961 1962
Mirror, mirror	Pinkerton's Assorted Colours	1966
Miss you	Jimmy Young	1963
Misty	Johnny Mathis	1960
Mockin' Bird Hill	Migil 5	1964
Monday Monday	Mamas & Papas	1966
Money	Bern Elliott & The Fenmen	1963 1964
Monsieur Dupont	Sandie Shaw	1969
Mony Mony	Tommy James & The Shondells	1968
Moody river	Pat Boone	1961
Moon river	Danny Williams	1961 1962
More and more party pops	Russ Conway	1960
More than I can say	Bobby Vee	1961
More than love	Ken Dodd	1966
Morningtown ride	Seekers	1966 1967
Move over darling	Doris Day	1964
Mr.Custer	Charlie Drake	1960
Mr.Tambourine man	Byrds	1965
Mrs. Mills medley	Mrs. Mills	1962
Mrs.Robinson	Simon & Garfunkel	1968 1969
Multiplication	Bobby Darin	1962
Muskrat	Everly Brothers	1961
Must be Madison	Joe Loss & His Orchestra	1962
My boomerang won't come back	Charlie Drake	1961
My boy lollipop	Millie	1964

Title	Artist	Year
My cherie amour	Stevie Wonder	1969
My friend the sea	Petula Clark	1961 1962
My generation	Who	1965 1966
My girl	Otis Redding	1966
My guy	Mary Wells	1964
My heart	Gene Vincent	1960
My heart has a mind of its own	Connie Francis	1960 1961
My kind of girl	Matt Monro	1961
My little girl	Crickets	1963
My little lady	Tremeloes	1968
My love	Petula Clark	1966
My love for you	Johnny Mathis	1960 1961
My mind's eye	Small Faces	1966 1967
My name is Jack	Manfred Mann	1968
My old man's a dustman	Lonnie Donegan	1960
My sentimental friend	Herman's Hermits	1969
My ship is coming in	Walker Brothers	1965 1966
My way	Frank Sinatra	1969
Mystery girl	Jess Conrad	1961
Natural born boogie	Humble Pie	1969
Needles and pins	Searchers	1964
Never goodbye	Karl Denver	1962
New Orleans	Gary U.S.Bonds	1961
New York mining disaster 1941	Bee Gees	1967
Nice 'n' easy	Frank Sinatra	1960
Night of fear	Move	1967
Night of the long grass	Troggs	1967
Nights in white satin	Moody Blues	1968
Nine times out of ten	Cliff Richard	1960
No arms could ever hold you	Bachelors	1964 1965
No milk today	Herman's Hermits	1966
No one can make my sunshine smile	Everly Brothers	1962
No particluar place to go	Chuck Berry	1964

Nobody I know	Peter & Gordon	1964
Nobody needs your love	Gene Pitney	1966
Nobody's child	Karen Young	1969
Nobody's darlin' but mine	Frank Ifield	1963
Non ho l'eta per amarti	Gigliola Cinquetti	1964
Not fade away	Rolling Stones	1964
Not responsible	Tom Jones	1966
Not too little - not too much	Chris Sandford	1963 1964
Not until the next time	Jim Reeves	1965
Nothing come easy	Sandie Shaw	1966
Nut rocker	B.Bumble & The Stingers	1962
Ob-la-di, ob-la-da	Bedrocks	1969
Ob-la-di, ob-la-da	Marmalade	1968 1969
Ode to Billie Joe	Bobbie Gentry	1967
Oh Carol	Neil Sedaka	1960
Oh happy day	Edwin Hawkins Singers	1969
Oh no not my baby	Manfred Mann	1965
Oh pretty woman	Roy Orbison	1964
Oh well	Fleetwood Mac	1969
Oh, lonesome me	Craig Douglas	1962
Okay!	Dave Dee, Dozy, Beaky, Mick & Tich	1967
Ol' MacDonald	Frank Sinatra	1960 1961
On a carousel	Hollies	1967
On a slow boat to China	Emile Ford & The Checkmates	1960
On my word	Cliff Richard	1965
On the beach	Cliff Richard	1964
On the rebound	Floyd Cramer	1961
On the road again	Canned Heat	1968
Once there was a time	Tom Jones	1966
Once upon a dream	Billy Fury	1962
One broken heart for sale	Elvis Presley	1963
One more dance	Esther & Abi Ofarim	1968
One road	Love Affair	1969
One way love	Cliff Bennett & The Rebel Rousers	1964
Only one woman	Marbles	1968

Only the lonely	Roy Orbison	1960
Opus 17 (Don't you worry 'bout me)	Four Seasons	1966
Our favourite melodies	Craig Douglas	1962
Out of time	Chris Farlowe	1966
Over under sideways down	Yardbirds	1966
Over you	Freddie & The Dreamers	1964
Paint it black	Rolling Stones	1966
Palisades Park	Freddy Cannon	1962
Pamela, Pamela	Wayne Fontana	1967
Paper roses	Kaye Sisters	1960
Paper sun	Traffic	1967
Paperback writer	Beatles	1966
Paradise lost	Herd	1968
Pasadena	Temperance Seven	1961
Passing breeze	Russ Conway	1960
Passing strangers	Sarah Vaughan & Billy Eckstine	1969
Peaceful	Georgie Fame	1969
Peek-a-boo	New Vaudeville Band	1967
Penny Lane	Beatles	1967
People	Tymes	1969
Pepe	Duane Eddy	1961
Pepe	Russ Conway	1961
Perfidia	Ventures	1960 1961
Piano party	Winifred Atwell	1960
Pick a bale of cotton	Lonnie Donegan	1962
Pictures of Lily	Who	1967
Pictures of matchstick men	Status Quo	1968
Piltdown rides again	Piltdown Men	1961
Pinball wizard	Who	1969
Pipeline	Chantays	1963
Pistol packin' mama	Gene Vincent	1960
Pleasant Valley Sundays	Monkees	1967
Please don't go	Donald Peers	1969
Please don't tease	Cliff Richard	1960
Please help me I'm falling	Hank Locklin	1960
Please please me	Beatles	1963
Poetry in motion	Johnny Tillotson	1960 1961

Poor man's son	Rockin' Berries	1965
Poor me	Adam Faith	1960
Pop go the workers	Barron Knights	1965
Pop goes the weasel	Anthony Newley	1961
Portrait of my love	Matt Monro	1961
Positively 4th Street	Bob Dylan	1965 1966
Pretty blue eyes	Craig Douglas	1960
Pretty flamingo	Manfred Mann	1966
Pretty paper	Roy Orbison	1964 1965
Princess in rags	Gene Pitney	1965 1966
Private number	Judy Clay & William Bell	1968 1969
Promises	Ken Dodd	1966
Proud Mary	Creedence Clearwater Revival	1969
Puppet on a string	Sandie Shaw	1967
Purple haze	Jimi Hendrix Experience	1967
Put your head on my shoulder	Paul Anka	1960
Put yourself in my place	Isley Brothers	1969
Quarter to three	Gary U.S.Bonds	1961
Quick Joey Small (run Joey run)	Kasenetz-Katz Singing Orchestral Circus	1969
Race with the devil	Gun	1968 1969
Rag doll	Four Seasons	1964
Ragamuffin man	Manfred Mann	1969
Rainbow valley	Love Affair	1968
Rainy day women no's 12 and 35	Bob Dylan	1966
Ramblin' Rose	Nat 'King' Cole	1962
Ramona	Bachelors	1964
Rawhide	Frankie Laine	1960
Reach for the stars	Shirley Bassey	1961
Reach out I'll be there	Four Tops	1966 1967
Red River rock	Johnny & The Hurricanes	1960
Reflections	Diana Ross & The Supremes	1967
Release me	Engelbert Humperdinck	1967
Remember (walkin' in the sand)	Shangri-La's	1964

Title	Artist	Year
Reminiscing	Buddy Holly	1962
Rescue me	Fontella Bass	1965 1966
Respect	Aretha Franklin	1967
Return of Django	Upsetters	1969
Return to sender	Elvis Presley	1962 1963
Reveille rock	Johnny & The Hurricanes	1960
Rhythm of the rain	Cascades	1963
Riders in the sky	Ramrods	1961
Right, said Fred	Bernard Cribbins	1962
Ring of fire	Duane Eddy	1961
River deep, mountain high	Ike & Tina Turner	1966
River, stay 'way from my door	Frank Sinatra	1960
Road runner	Jr. Walker & The Allstars	1969
Robot	Tornados	1963
Robot man	Connie Francis	1960
Rock around the clock	Bill Haley & His Comets	1968
Rock-a-hula baby	Elvis Presley	1962
Rockin' around the Christmas tree	Brenda Lee	1962 1963
Rocking goose	Johnny & The Hurricanes	1960 1961
Romeo	Petula Clark	1961
Roses are red (my love)	Bobby Vinton	1962
Roses are red (my love)	Ronnie Carroll	1962
Roses of Picardy	Vince Hill	1967
Rosie	Don Partridge	1968
Royal event	Russ Conway	1960
Rubber ball	Bobby Vee	1961
Rubber ball	Marty Wilde	1961
Ruby, don't take your love to town	Kenny Rogers & The First Edition	1969
Run to him	Bobby Vee	1962
Runaround Sue	Dion	1961
Runaway	Del Shannon	1961
Runnin' scared	Roy Orbison	1961
Running bear	Johnny Preston	1960
Sabre dance	Love Scultpture	1968 1969
Sailor	Anne Shelton	1961

Sailor	Petula Clark	1961
Samantha	Kenny Ball & His Jazzmen	1961
San Franciscan nights	Eric Burdon	1967
San Francisco (Be sure to wear some flowers in your hair)	Scott McKenzie	1967
Save me	Dave Dee, Dozy, Beaky Mick & Tich	1966 1967
Save the last dance for me	Drifters	1960 1961
Saved by the bell	Robin Gibb	1969
Say I won't be there	Springfields	1963
Say wonderful things	Ronnie Carroll	1963
Scarlett O'Hara	Jet Harris & Tony Meehan	1963
Sea of heartbreak	Don Gibson	1961
Sealed with a kiss	Brian Hyland	1962
Searchin'	Hollies	1963
Second hand Rose	Barbra Streisand	1966
Secret love	Kathy Kirby	1963 1964
See Emily play	Pink Floyd	1967
See my friend	Kinks	1965
Semi-detached suburban Mr.James	Manfred Mann	1966
Set me free	Kinks	1965
Seven drunken nights	Dubliners	1967
Seven little girls (sitting in the back seat)	Avons	1960
Seven rooms of gloom	Four Tops	1967
Sha la la	Manfred Mann	1964
Sha la la la lee	Small Faces	1966
Shakin' all over	Johnny Kidd & The Pirates	1960
Shapes of things	Yardbirds	1966
Sharing you	Bobby Vee	1962
Shazam	Duane Eddy	1960
She loves you	Beatles	1963 1964
She wears my ring	Solomon King	1968
She'd rather be with me	Turtles	1967
Sheila	Tommy Roe	1962
Sherry	Four Seasons	1962
She's about a mover	Sir Douglas Quintet	1965

She's not there	Zombies	1964
She's not you	Elvis Presley	1962
Shindig	Shadows	1963
Shortnin' bread	Viscounts	1960
Shotgun wedding	Roy 'C'	1966
Shout	Lulu & The Luvvers	1964
Show me girl	Herman's Hermits	1964
Silence is golden	Tremeloes	1967
Silhouettes	Herman's Hermits	1965
Simon says	1910 Fruitgum Company	1968
Simon Smith and the amazing dancing bear	Alan Price Set	1967
Single girl	Sandy Posey	1967
Sitting in the park	Georgie Fame	1967
Sixteen reasons	Connie Stevens	1960
Sleepy Joe	Herman's Hermits	1968
Sloop John B	Beach Boys	1966
Snoopy vs The Red Baron	Royal Guardsmen	1967
Snow coach	Russ Conway	1960
So do I	Kenny Ball & His Jazzmen	1962
So long baby	Del Shannon	1961 1962
So sad	Everly Brothers	1960
Softly as I leave you	Matt Monro	1962
Some day we're gonna love again	Searchers	1964
Some kinda fun	Chris Montez	1963
Some kind-a-earthquake	Duane Eddy	1960
Some of your lovin'	Dusty Springfield	1965
Somebody else's girl	Billy Fury	1963
Somebody help me	Spencer Davis Group	1966
Someday one day	Seekers	1966
Someone else's baby	Adam Faith	1960
Someone, someone	Brian Poole & The Tremeloes	1964
Somethin' stupid	Nancy Sinatra & Frank Sinatra	1967
Something	Beatles	1969
Something here in my heart	Paper Dolls	1968
Something in the air	Thunderclap Newman	1969
Something's gotten hold of my heart	Gene Pitney	1967 1968

Something's happening	Herman's Hermits	1969
Somewhere	P.J.Proby	1964
		1965
Somewhere in the country	Gene Pitney	1968
Somewhere my love	Mike Sammes Singers	1967
Son of a preacher man	Dusty Springfield	1968
		1969
Son, this is she	John Leyton	1962
Sorrow	Merseys	1966
Sorry Suzanne	Hollies	1969
Soul sister, brown sugar	Sam & Dave	1969
Sound of silence	Bachelors	1966
Space oddity	David Bowie	1969
Spanish flea	Herb Alpert & The Tijuana Brass	1966
Spanish Harlem	Jimmy Justice	1962
Speak to me pretty	Brenda Lee	1962
Speedy Gonzales	Pat Boone	1962
Staccato's theme	Elmer Bernstein	1960
Stairway to heaven	Neil Sedaka	1960
Standing in the shadows of love	Four Tops	1967
Standing on the corner	King Brothers	1960
Starry eyed	Michael Holliday	1960
Stay	Hollies	1963
		1964
Stay	Maurice Williams & The Zodiacs	1961
Stay awhile	Dusty Springfield	1964
Staying in	Bobby Vee	1961
Step inside love	Cilla Black	1968
Still	Karl Denver	1963
Still I'm sad	Yardbirds	1965
Stingray	Shadows	1965
Stop her on sight	Edwin Starr	1969
Stop stop stop	Hollies	1966
Stop! In the name of love	Supremes	1965
Strange brew	Cream	1967
Stranger on the shore	Mr. Acker Bilk & His Paramount Jazz Band	1961
		1962
Strangers in the night	Frank Sinatra	1966

Strawberry fair	Anthony Newley	1960 1961
Strawberry Fields forever	Beatles	1967
Stuck on you	Elvis Presley	1960
Substitute	Who	1966
Subterranean homesick blues	Bob Dylan	1965
Such a night	Elvis Presley	1964
Sucu sucu	Laurie Johnson Orchestra	1961
Suddenly you love me	Tremeloes	1968
Sugar and spice	Searchers	1963
Sugar sugar	Archies	1969
Sugar town	Nancy Sinatra	1967
Sukiyaki	Kenny Ball & His Jazzmen	1963
Sukiyaki	Kyu Sakamoto	1963
Summer holiday	Cliff Richard	1963
Summer in the city	Lovin' Spoonful	1966
Summer nights	Marianne Faithfull	1965
Summer set	Mr.Acker Bilk & His Paramount Jazz Band	1960
Sun arise	Rolf Harris	1962 1963
Sunny	Bobby Hebb	1966
Sunny	Georgie Fame	1966
Sunny afternoon	Kinks	1966
Sunshine girl	Herman's Hermits	1968
Sunshine Superman	Donovan	1966 1967
Supergirl	Graham Bonney	1966
Surrender	Elvis Presley	1961
Surround yourself with sorrow	Cilla Black	1969
Susannah's still alive	Dave Davies	1968
Suspicious minds	Elvis Presley	1969
Sway	Bobby Rydell	1961
Sweet dream	Jethro Tull	1969
Sweet nothin's	Brenda Lee	1960
Sweet soul music	Arthur Conley	1967
Sweets for my sweet	Searchers	1963
Swinging on a star	Big Dee Irwin	1963 1964
Take five	Dave Brubeck Quartet	1961

Take good care of my baby	Bobby Vee	1961 1962
Take me for what I'm worth	Searchers	1966
Take me in your arms and love me	Gladys Knight & The Pips	1967
Take me to your heart again	Vince Hill	1966
Take these chains from my heart	Ray Charles	1963
Tears	Ken Dodd	1965 1966
Teen beat	Sandy Nelson	1960
Tell him	Billie Davis	1963
Tell Laura I love her	Ricky Valance	1960
Tell me what he said	Helen Shapiro	1962
Tell me when	Applejacks	1964
Tell me why	Elvis Presley	1965
Telstar	Tornados	1962 1963
Temptation	Everly Brothers	1961
Teresa	Joe Dolan	1969
Terry	Twinkle	1964 1965
Thank u very much	Scaffold	1967 1968
That girl belongs to yesterday	Gene Pitney	1964
That's my home	Mr Acker Bilk & His Paramount Jazz Band	1961
That's love	Billy Fury	1960
That's nice	Neil Christian	1966
That's the way	Honeycombs	1965
That's the way God planned it	Billy Preston	1969
That's what love will do	Joe Brown	1963
That's you	Nat 'King' Cole	1960
The ballad of Bonnie and Clyde	Georgie Fame	1968
The ballad of John and Yoko	Beatles	1969
The boat that I row	Lulu	1967
The boxer	Simon & Garfunkel	1969
The carnival is over	Seekers	1965 1966
The clapping song	Shirley Ellis	1965
The Comancheros	Lonnie Donegan	1962
The cruel sea	Dakotas	1963

The crying game	Dave Berry	1964
The day I met Marie	Cliff Richard	1967
The end of the world	Skeeter Davis	1963
The first cut is the deepest	P.P.Arnold	1967
The first time	Adam Faith	1963
The folk singer	Tommy Roe	1963
The frightened city	Shadows	1961
The game of love	Wayne Fontana & The Mindbenders	1965
The good, the bad, and the ugly	Hugo Montenegro	1968 1969
The green leaves of summer	Kenny Ball & His Jazzmen	1962
The happening	Supremes	1967
The heart of a teenage girl	Craig Douglas	1960
The house that Jack built	Alan Price Set	1967
The Ice Cream man	Tornados	1963
The Israelites	Desmond Dekker & The Aces	1969
The language of love	John D.Loudermilk	1962
The last time	Rolling Stones	1965
The last waltz	Engelbert Humperdinck	1967 1968
The legend of Xanadu	Dave Dee, Dozy, Beaky, Mick & Tich	1968
The letter	Box Tops	1967
The lion sleeps tonight (Wimoweh)	Tokens	1962
The Liquidator	Harry J. & The All Stars	1969
The loco-motion	Little Eva	1962
The main attraction	Pat Boone	1962 1963
The Mighty Quinn	Manfred Mann	1968
The minute you're gone	Cliff Richard	1965
The more I see you	Chris Montez	1966
The next time	Cliff Richard	1962 1963
The night has a thousand eyes	Bobby Vee	1963
The onion song	Marvin Gaye & Tammi Terrell	1969
The other man's grass (is always greener)	Petula Clark	1968

171

The party's over	Lonnie Donegan	1962
The Pied Piper	Crispian St.Peters	1966
The price of love	Everly Brothers	1965
The red balloon	Dave Clark Five	1968
The rise and fall of Flingel Bunt	Shadows	1964
The river	Ken Dodd	1965 1966
The savage	Shadows	1961 1962
The shrine on the second floor	Cliff Richard & The Shadows	1960
The son of Hickory Holler's tramp	O.C.Smith	1968
The special years	Val Doonican	1965
The stranger	Shadows	1960 1961
The sun ain't gonna shine anymore	Walker Brothers	1966
The Swiss maid	Del Shannon	1962 1963
The time has come	Adam Faith	1961
The times they are a changin'	Bob Dylan	1965
The tracks of my tears	Smokey Robinson & The Miracles	1969
The twelfth of never	Cliff Richard	1964
The twist	Chubby Checker	1962
The urge	Freddy Cannon	1960
The wanderer	Dion & The Belmonts	1962
The way it used to be	Engelbert Humperdinck	1969
The wayward wind	Frank Ifield	1963
The wedding	Julie Rogers	1964
The wind cries Mary	Jimi Hendrix Experience	1967
The windmills of your mind	Noel Harrison	1969
The wreck of the Antoinette	Dave Dee, Dozy, Beaky, Mick & Tich	1968
The young ones	Cliff Richard	1962
Them there eyes	Emile Ford & The Checkmates	1960
Theme for a dream	Cliff Richard	1961
Theme for young lovers	Shadows	1964
Theme from 'A Summer Place'	Percy Faith	1960
Theme from Dixie	Duane Eddy	1961
Theme from 'Dr.Kildare'	Johnny Spence	1962

Theme from 'Dr.Kildare' (Three stars will shine tonight)	Richard Chamberlain	1962
Theme from 'Exodus'	Ferrante & Teicher	1961
Theme from 'James Bond'	John Barry Orchestra	1962
Theme from 'Maigret'	Joe Loss & His Orchestra	1962
Theme from 'The Legion's Last Patrol'	Ken Thorne	1963
Theme from 'The Man With The Golden Arm'	Jet Harris	1962
Theme from 'Z-Cars'	Johnny Keating Orchestra	1962
Then he kissed me	Crystals	1963
Then I kissed her	Beach Boys	1967
There but for fortune	Joan Baez	1965
There goes my everything	Engelbert Humperdinck	1967
There is a mountain	Donovan	1967
There must be a way	Frankie Vaughan	1967 1968
There won't be many coming home	Roy Orbison	1966 1967
There's a heartache following me	Jim Reeves	1964 1965
There's a kind of hush	Herman's Hermits	1967
These boots are made for walkin'	Nancy Sinatra	1966
They're coming to take me away, ha ha!	Napoleon XIV	1966
Things	Bobby Darin	1962
This door swings both ways	Herman's Hermits	1966
This golden ring	Fortunes	1966
This guy's in love with you	Herb Alpert	1968
This is it	Adam Faith	1961
This is my song	Harry Secombe	1967
This is my song	Petula Clark	1967
This little bird	Marianne Faithfull	1965
This old heart of mine	Isley Brothers	1968 1969
This wheel's on fire	Julie Driscoll, Brian Auger & The Trinity	1968
Those were the days	Mary Hopkin	1968
Three bells	Brian Poole & The Tremeloes	1965
Three steps to heaven	Eddie Cochran	1960
Throw down a line	Cliff Richard	1969

Ticket to ride	Beatles	1965
Tie me kangaroo down	Rolf Harris	1960
Till the end of the day	Kinks	1965
		1966
Time	Craig Douglas	1961
Time drags by	Cliff Richard	1966
Time is tight	Booker T & The MG's	1969
Tin soldier	Small Faces	1967
		1968
Tired of waiting for you	Kinks	1965
To know you is to love you	Peter & Gordon	1965
To love somebody	Nina Simone	1969
To whom it concerns	Chris Andrews	1965
		1966
Tobacco Road	Nashville Teens	1964
Together	Connie Francis	1961
Together	P.J.Proby	1964
Tokyo melody	Helmut Zacharias	1964
Tomorrow	Sandie Shaw	1966
Too busy thinking 'bout my baby	Marvin Gaye	1969
Too good	Little Tony	1960
Too soon to know	Roy Orbison	1966
Tossing and turning	Ivy League	1965
Touch me, touch me	Dave Dee, Dozy, Beaky, Mick & Tich	1967
Tower of strength	Frankie Vaughan	1961
		1962
Toy balloons	Russ Conway	1961
		1962
Tracy	Cufflinks	1969
Trains and boats and planes	Billy J.Kramer & The Dakotas	1965
Trains and boats and planes	Burt Bacharach	1965
Tramp	Otis Redding & Carla Thomas	1967
Travellin' light	Cliff Richard & The Shadows	1960
Travellin' Man	Ricky Nelson	1961
True love ways	Peter & Gordon	1965
Twenty four hours from Tulsa	Gene Pitney	1963
		1964
Twist and shout	Brian Poole & The Tremeloes	1963
Twistin' the night away	Sam Cooke	1962

Two kinds of teardrops	Del Shannon	1963
Two little boys	Rolf Harris	1969
U.S.Male	Elvis Presley	1968
Um, um, um, um, um, um	Wayne Fontana & The Mindbenders	1964
Unchained melody	Righteous Brothers	1965
Under new management	Barron Knights	1966 1967
Universal	Small Faces	1968
Unsquare dance	Dave Brubeck	1962
Until it's time for you to go	Four Pennies	1965
Up on the roof	Kenny Lynch	1963
Up, up and away	Johnny Mann Singers	1967
Uptight (everything's alright)	Stevie Wonder	1966
V.A.C.A.T.I.O.N.	Connie Francis	1962
Valleri	Monkees	1968
Valley of tears	Buddy Holly	1961
Venus in blue jeans	Mark Wynter	1962
Visions	Cliff Richard	1966
Viva Bobby Joe	Equals	1969
Viva Las Vegas	Elvis Presley	1964
Walk away	Matt Monro	1964
Walk away Renee	Four Tops	1967 1968
Walk don't run	John Barry Seven	1960
Walk don't run	Ventures	1960
Walk in the Black Forest	Horst Jankowski	1965
Walk like a man	Four Seasons	1963
Walk on by	Dionne Warwick	1964
Walk on by	Leroy Van Dyke	1962
Walk right back	Everly Brothers	1961
Walk right in	Rooftop Singers	1963
Walk tall	Val Doonican	1964 1965
Walk with me	Seekers	1966
Walking back to happiness	Helen Shapiro	1961 1962
Walking to New Orleans	Fats Domino	1960
War Lord	Shadows	1965 1966
War paint	Brook Brothers	1961

Waterloo sunset	Kinks	1967
Way down yonder in New Orleans	Freddy Cannon	1960
Way of life	Family Dogg	1969
We are in love	Adam Faith	1964
We can work it out	Beatles	1965 1966
We can work it out	Beatles	1965
We gotta get out of this place	Animals	1965
We love you	Rolling Stones	1967
Weekend	Eddie Cochran	1961
Welcome to my world	Jim Reeves	1963
Well I ask you	Eden Kane	1961
We're gonna go fishin'	Hank Locklin	1963
We're through	Hollies	1964
Wet dream	Max Romeo	1969
What a mouth	Tommy Steele	1960
What a wonderful world	Louis Armstrong	1968
What becomes of the broken-hearted?	Jimmy Ruffin	1966 1967
What do you want to make those eyes at me for?	Emile Ford & The Checkmates	1960
What do you want?	Adam Faith	1960
What does it take (to win your love)?	Jr.Walker & The Allstars	1969
What have they done to the rain?	Searchers	1964 1965
What in the world's come over you?	Jack Scott	1960
What is a man?	Four Tops	1969
What now my love	Sonny & Cher	1966
What now my love?	Shirley Bassey	1962
What would I be?	Val Doonican	1966 1967
Whatcha gonna do about it	Small Faces	1965
What'd I say	Jerry Lee Lewis	1961
What's new pussycat?	Tom Jones	1965
Wheels	String-a-longs	1961
When a man loves a woman	Percy Sledge	1966
When I come home	Spencer Davis Group	1966

When Johnny comes marching home	Adam Faith	1960
When my little girl is smiling	Craig Douglas	1962
When my little girl is smiling	Jimmy Justice	1962
When the girl in your arms is the girl in your heart	Cliff Richard	1961
When two worlds collide	Jim Reeves	1969
When will I be loved	Everly Brothers	1960
When will the good apples fall	Seekers	1967
When will you say I love you	Billy Fury	1963
When you walk in the room	Searchers	1964
When you're young and in love	Marvelettes	1967
Where are you now (my love)	Jackie Trent	1965
Where did our love go?	Supremes	1964
Where do you go to (my lovely)	Peter Sarstedt	1969
Where the boys are	Connie Francis	1961
Where will you be?	Sue Nicholls	1968
Whispering	Bachelors	1963
Whispering	Nino Tempo & April Stevens	1964
White horses	Jackie	1968
Who am I	Adam Faith	1961
Who could be bluer?	Jerry Lordan	1960
Why	Anthony Newley	1960
Why	Frankie Avalon	1960
Wichita lineman	Glen Campbell	1969
Wild in the country	Elvis Presley	1961
Wild one	Bobby Rydell	1960
Wild thing	Troggs	1966
Wild wind	John Leyton	1961
Will I what?	Mike Sarne	1962
Will you still love me tomorrow?	Shirelles	1961
Wimoweh	Karl Denver	1962
Winchester Cathedral	New Vaudeville Band	1966
Wind me up (let me go)	Cliff Richard	1965 1966
Winter world of love	Engelbert Humperdinck	1969
Wipe out	Surfaris	1963
Wishin' and hopin'	Merseybeats	1964
Wishing	Buddy Holly	1963
With a girl like you	Troggs	1966
With a little help from my friends	Joe Cocker	1968

With a little help from my friends	Young Idea	1967
With the eyes of a child	Cliff Richard	1969
With these hands	Tom Jones	1965
Without love	Tom Jones	1969
Wonderful land	Shadows	1962
Wonderful world	Herman's Hermits	1965
Wonderful world of the young	Danny Williams	1962
Wonderful world, beautiful people	Jimmy Cliff	1969
Wooden heart	Elvis Presley	1961
Wooly bully	Sam The Sham & The Pharoahs	1965
Words	Bee Gees	1968
Working in the coal mine	Lee Dorsey	1966
World	Bee Gees	1967 1968
Ya Ya twist	Petula Clark	1962
Yeh yeh	Georgie Fame	1964 1965
Yellow submarine	Beatles	1966
Yes I will	Hollies	1965
Yes my darling daughter	Eydie Gorme	1962
Yesterday	Matt Monro	1965
Yesterday has gone	Cupid's Inspiration	1968
Yesterday man	Chris Andrews	1965 1966
Yester-me, yester-you, yesterday	Stevie Wonder	1969
You always hurt the one you love	Clarence 'Frogman' Henry	1961
You can never stop me loving you	Kenny Lynch	1963
You can't hurry love	Supremes	1966
You don't have to be a baby to cry	Caravelles	1963
You don't have to say you love me	Dusty Springfield	1966
You don't know	Helen Shapiro	1961
You don't know me	Ray Charles	1962
You got soul	Johnny Nash	1969
You got what it takes	Marv Johnson	1960
You keep me hangin' on	Supremes	1966 1967

You keep me hanging on	Vanilla Fudge	1967
You know what I mean	Vernons Girls	1962
You must have been a beautiful baby	Bobby Darin	1961
You only live twice	Nancy Sinatra / Nancy Sinatra & Lee Hazlewood	1967
You really got me	Kinks	1964
You were made for me	Freddie & The Dreamers	1963 1964
You were on my mind	Crispian St.Peters	1966
You won't be leavin'	Herman's Hermits	1966
You're no good	Swinging Blue Jeans	1964
You'll answer to me	Cleo Laine	1961
You'll never get to heaven (if you break my heart)	Dionne Warwick	1964
You'll never know	Shirley Bassey	1961
You'll never know what you're missing	Emile Ford & The Checkmates	1960
You'll never walk alone	Gerry & The Pacemakers	1963 1964
Young girl	Gary Puckett & The Union Gap	1968
Young lovers	Paul & Paula	1963
Young world	Ricky Nelson	1962
Your cheating heart	Ray Charles	1963
Your mother should know	Beatles	1967 1968
You're all I need to get by	Marvin Gaye & Tammi Terrell	1968
You're breakin' my heart	Keely Smith	1965
You're driving me crazy	Temperance Seven	1961
You're my world	Cilla Black	1964
You're sixteen	Johnny Burnette	1961
You're the one	Kathy Kirby	1964
You're the only good thing (that happened to me)	Jim Reeves	1961 1962
You've got your troubles	Fortunes	1965
You've lost that lovin' feelin'	Cilla Black	1965
You've lost that lovin' feelin'	Righteous Brothers	1965 1969

You've not changed	Sandie Shaw	1967
Yummy yummy yummy	Ohio Express	1968
Zabadak!	Dave Dee, Dozy, Beaky, Mick & Tich	1967
Zorba's dance	Marcello Minerbi	1965

References:

[1] "Announcement of the christening of Lady Louise Windsor". *The official website of The British Monarchy*. The Royal Household. 8 April 2004. Retrieved 2012-01-27

[2] "Margaret weds Armstrong-Jones". *On This Day* (BBC). 6 May 1960. Archived from the original on 7 March 2008. Retrieved 2008-02-11

[3] Science Museum (London) display

[4] Palmer, Alan; Veronica (1992). *The Chronology of British History*. London: Century Ltd. ISBN 0-7126-5616-2

[5] The intended last day was 17 November. Vinen, Richard (2014). *National Service: Conscription in Britain, 1945-1963*. London: Allen Lane. p.361. ISBN 978-1-846-14387-8

[6] http://en.wikipedia.org/wiki/1960_in_the_United_Kingdom

[7] "Thirty years on from the first £1m transfer Sportsmail looks at the record-breakers". *Daily Mail* (London). 6 February 2009. Retrieved 2010-02-08

[8] "Broadcasting of the Grand National". *Aintree.co.uk*. Retrieved 2011-03-11

[9] "Burnley Wins English Soccer". *The Age* (Melbourne). 4 May 1960. Retrieved 2012-01-27

[10] "1960". Fa-cupfinals.co.uk. Archived from the original on 19 April 2012. Retrieved 4 December 2010

[11] "Vic Wilson". *Wisden Cricketers' Almanack*. John Wisden & Co. 2009. Retrieved 2009-12-21

[12] Hill, Tim (2007). *Then There Was Music: The Beatles*. London: Daily Mail. p.13. ISBN 0-9545267-7-5

[13] McKay, George (2005). "New Orleans jazz, protest (Aldermaston) and carnival (Beaulieu)". *Circular Breathing: the Cultural Politics of Jazz in Britain*. Durham, NC: Duke University Press. ISBN 0-8223-3560-3

[14] "The day when traditional jazz caused a riot". *The Observer* (London) 29 July 2012. p.6 (The New Review).

[15] *Penguin Pocket On This Day*. Penguin Reference Library. 2006. ISBN 0-14-102715-0

[16] "Lady Chatterley's Lover sold out". *On This Day* (BBC). 10 November 1960. Retrieved 2008-02-11

[17] http://en-wikipedia.org/wiki/1960_in_British_music

[18] Obituary: "Adam Faith", *The Guardian*, 10 March 2003

[19] "1958: Historic Sheerness docks to close". *BBC News*. 20 February 2009. Retrieved 30 September 2011

[20] *Liberal Democrat News* 15 October 2010

[21] Challoner, Jack, ed. (2009) *1001 Inventions That Changed the World*. London. Cassell. pp. 676-7. ISBN 978-1-84403-611-0

[22] Cole, T.C. (1970). *Bluebell Railway – Steaming On!* Sheffield Park: Bluebell Railway.

[23] Ingall, Tom (8 October 2010). "Fiftieth anniversary of the end of trams in Sheffield". BBC. Retrieved 2011-01-16

[24] "English Premier League 1960/1961". *Tottenham Hotspur Mad*. Retrieved 2 March 2011

[25] "Tottenham Hotspur results 1960/1961". *Tottenham Hotspur Mad*. Retrieved 2 March 2011

[26] "Dramatic End to Britain's Memorable Wimbledon". *The Times* (London). 10 July 1961 p.3.

[27] http://en.wikipedia.org/wiki/1961_in_the_United_Kingdom

[28] "Key Dates". Royal Shakespeare Company. 2010. Archived from the original on 16 June 2010. Retrieved 30 June 2010

[29] https://en/wikipedia.org/wiki/1961_in_music

[30] "Special events in the development of women's equality". Catherine of Siena Virtual College. Retrieved 1 February 2011

[31] "The Computer Centre Opens". *Spread Eagle:* 252. 1961

[32] Barclays Group Archives. *Barclays Fact Sheet: Principal Events, 2.*

[33] *Penguin Pocket On This Day*. Penguin Reference Library. 2006. ISBN 0-14-102715-0

[34] Palmer, Alan; Veronica (1992). *The Chronology of British History*. London: Century Ltd. ISBN 0-7126-5616-2

[35] "Ratification of the Convention on the OECD". Archived from the original on 17 September 2009. Retrieved 14 September 2009
[36] "Panda replaced zebra at road crossing". *BBC News*. 14 June 1961. Retrieved 30 March 2012
[37] "1961". *Those were the days. Express & Star*. Retrieved 30 March 2012
[38] "1962: To the brink of war…". Wolverhampton: Express & Star
[39] Waugh, William (1990). *John Charnley: Th Man and the Hip*. London: Springer-Verlag. pp. 122-4. ISBN 3-540-19587-4.
[40] Burnton, Simon (6 March 2010). "6 March 1962: Accrington Stanley resigns from the Football League". *The Guardian* (London).
[41] http://en.wikipedia.org/wiki/1962_in_the_United_Kingdom
[42] https://en.wikipedia.org/wiki/1962_in_British_Music
[43] Spitz, Bob (2005). *The Beatles: The Biography*. New York: Little, Brown. ISBN 978-0-316-80352-6.
[44] Palmer. Alan; Veronica (1992). *The Chronology of British History*. London: Century Ltd. pp. 419-420. ISBN 0-7126-5616-2.
[45] "Dr. No (1962)". *MI6*. Retrieved 2010-09-01.
[46] Smith, Alan. 50s & 60s UK Charts – The Truth!" *Dave McAleer's website*. Retrieved 4 November 2010.
[47] *Penguin Pocket On This Day*. Penguin Reference Library. 2006. ISBN 0-14-102715-02
[48] Harrison, Ian (2003). *The Book of Firsts*. London: Cassell. p.45. ISBN 1-84403-201-9.
[49] "Safeway takeover completed". *Daily Mail* (London). Retrieved 18 April 2011.
[50] Marshall, Prince (1972) *Wheels of London*. The Sunday Times Magazine. p. 109. ISBN 0-7230-0068-9.
[51] "Ford Cortina (1962-1982): a National Institution". *Yahoo! Cars*. Retrieved 2011-06-16.
[52] "1962". CBRD. Retrieved 2012-07-03.
[53] http://en.wikipedia.org/wiki/1963_in_the_United_Kingdom
[54] "1963: Train robbers make off with millions". *BBC News*. 8 August 1963. Archived from the original on 7 March 2008. Retrieved 2008-02-11
[55] "Everton FC History – Goodison Park 11th May 1963". *Bluekipper.com*. 2004. Retrieved 2011-04-27
[56] "1963". http://www.fa-cupfinals.co.uk/. Archived from the original on 27 April 2012
[57] https://en.wikipedia.org/wiki/1963_in_British_music
[58] "Sindy doll 'set to be a Christas hit". *National Newswire* (Press Association). 6 July 2006.
[59] Gillian, Lesley (22 November 2003). "The return of a living doll: The new look Sindy will cause collectors to rethink". *FT Weekend – Collecting (Financial Times). p.8.*
[60] *Sindy: Every little girl's dream comes true* (Vinyl back cover). Pedigree Dolls Ltd. 1963.
[61] "Polypropylene stacking chair – The Frederick Parker Collection". *Vads*. London Metropolitan University. Retrieved 2010-07-12
[62] Excell, Jon (2 October 2007). "This week in … 1963 – The Vauxhall Viva HA". *The Engineer* (London). Retrieved 2012-07-07.
[63] *Penguin Pocket On This Day*. Penguin Reference Library. 2006. ISBN 0-14-102715-0.
[64] "1963". *Cbrd*. Retrieved 2012-06-08.
[65] "City Status For Southampton". *The Times*. 12 February 1964. p.5.
[66] Palmer, Alan; Veronica (1992). *The Chronology of British History*. London: Century Ltd. pp 422-423. ISBN 978-0-7126-5616-0
[67] Hadfield, Charles; Norris, John (1968). *Waterways to Stratford* (2nd ed). Newton Abbot: David & Charles. ISBN 978-0-7153-4231-2
[68] On this day – 18 April 1964 – Liverpool FC
[69] McRobbie, Angela (1991). *Feminism and youth culture: from "Jackie" to "Just Seventeen"*. Basingstoke: Macmillan. ISBN 978-0-333-45263-9.
[70] *Penguin Pocket On This Day*. Penguin Reference Library. 2006. ISBN 978-0-14-102715-9.
[71] "Radio Sutch & City in Pictures & Audio Part 1. Bob Le-Roi. 31 March 2010. Archived from the original on 2013-05-20. Retrieved 2011-08-23.

[72] *A Hard Day's Night* at the Internet Movie Database
[73] http://en.wikipedia.org/wiki/1964_in_the_United_Kingdom
[74] https://en.wikipedia.org/wiki/1964_in_British_music
[75] "1964: Green light for Channel Tunnel". *BBC News*. 6 February 1964. Archived from the original on 4 December 2007. Retrieved 2008-01-10.
[76] Kennedy, Liam, ed. (2004). *Remaking Birmingham: The Visual Culture of Urban Regeneration*. Routledge Ltd. pp 17-18. ISBN 978-0-415-28839-2.
[77] "Our history". Hanson. Archived from the original on 28 September 2010. Retrieved 2010-10-05.
[78] Bullock, John (1993). *The Rootes Brothers: story of a motoring empire*. Sparkford: Patrick Stevens Ltd. p 228. ISBN 978-1-85260-454-7.
[79] Jack Galusha, "Daihatsu Sirion 1.0 S", *Autocar*, retrieved 2013-04-13 Archived April 3, 2012 at the Wayback Machine
[80] "Goldie the eagle evades capture again". *BBC News*. 7 March 1965. Retrieved 2008-01-15.
[81] http://en.wikipedia.org/wiki/1965_in_the_United_Kingdom
[82] Scott-Elliot, Robin (19 February 2010). "Old Trafford Centenary: 10 games that define "Theatre of Dreams". *The Independent* (London). Retrieved 2012-03-30.
[83] "1965". *Those were the days. Express & Star*. Retrieved 2012-03-30.
[84] "Live: Capitol Cinema, Cardiff". *The Beatles Bible*. 1965-12-12. Retrieved 2014-02-19.
[85] https://en.wikipedia.org/wiki/1965_in_British_music
[86] Beatles Bible
[87] "Corgi History". Retrieved 2010-08-17.
[88] "The 60's Mini Skirt Fashion History – Mary Quant". Retrieved 23 June 2010.
[89] Horton, Ros; Simmons, Sally (2007). *Women Who Changed the World*. Retrieved 23 June 2010.
[90] Miles, Barry (2009). *The British Invasion: the Music, the Times, the Era*. Sterling Publishing Company, Inc. Retrieved 23 June 2010.
[91] Hancock, Ciaran (2005-11-13). "Ireland Asda on the hunt for retail sites in Donegal and Louth". *The Times* (London). Retrieved 2011-04-18.
[92] Marr, Andrew (2007). *A History of Modern Britain*. London: Macmillan. p.248. ISBN 978-1-4050-0538-8.
[93] *Penguin Pocket On This Day*. Penguin Reference Library. 2006. ISBN 0-14-102715-0.
[94] *Penguin Pocket On This Day*. Penguin Reference Library. 2006. ISBN 0-14-102715-0
[95] "Title reclaimed after Chelsea win". *LiverpoolFCtv*. Retrieved 2011-05-03.
[96] "Football glory for England". *BBC News*. 30 July 1966. Archived from the original on 7 March 2008. Retrieved 2008-02-03.
[97] Revoir, Paul (7 October 2008). "The most watched TV shows of all time – and they are all old programmes". *Daily Mail*. Retrieved 2011-03-03.
[98] "Thirty years on from the first £1m transfer Sportsmail looks at the record-breakers". *Daily Mail*, February 2009, retrieved 2013-03-05.
[99] http://en.wikipedia.org/wiki/1966_in_the_United_Kingdom
[100] https://en.wikipedia.org/wiki/1966_in_British_music
[101] Blaney, John (2005). John Lennon: Listen to This Book (illustrated ed.). [S.1]: Paper Jukebox. p.5. ISBN 978-0-9544528-1-0. p.3.
[102] Palmer, Alan; Veronica (1992). *The Chronology of British History*. London: Century Ltd. pp 424-425. ISBN 0-7126-5616-2.
[103] "New Ford Cortina With More Room". *The Glasgow Herald*. 18 October 1966. p.6. Retrieved 2013-03-05.
[104] "Milton Keynes: the basics". Milton Keynes City Discovery Centre. Archived from the original on 20 July 2011. Retrieved 2011-09-01.
[105] The "North Buckinghamshire (Milton Keynes) New Town (Designation Order)"". *London Gazette*: 827. 24 January 1967.

[106] "New Town will be home for 250,000 Londoners: Plan for Buckinghamshire approved". *The Times* (56833) (London). 13 January 1967 p.9.
[107] "1967: First all-British satellite 2Ariel 3' launched". *BBC News*. 5 May 1967. Archived from the original on 17 December 2008. Retrieved 2009-01-22.
[108] "1967: De Gaulle says 'non' to Britain – again". *BBC News*. 27 November 1967. Archived from the original on 7 March 2008. Retrieved 2008-02-03.
[109] Baines, Mary. "History". St Christopher's. Retrieved 2012-08-08.
[110] http://en.wikipedia.org/wiki/1967_in_the_United_Kingdom
[111] "Manchester United take championship home to Old Trafford". *The Guardian*
[112] FA Cup Final 1967
[113] "1967: Sir Francis Chichester sails home". *BBC News*. 28 May 1967. Archived from the original on 7 March 2008. Retrieved 2008-02-03.
[114] "Britain's First Colour TV Programme". *British TV History*. Archived from the original on 27 October 2010. Retrieved 2010-10-05.
[115] "1967: Harold Wilson wins Moving apology". *BBC News*. 11 October 1967. Archived from the original on 7 March 2008. Retrieved 2008-02-03.
[116] "1967: Stones guitarist escapes jail for drugs". *BBC News*. 12 December 1967. Archived from the original on 7 March 2008. Retrieved 2008-02-03.
[117] https://en.wikipedia.org/wiki/1967_in_British_music
[118] https://en.wikipedia.org/wiki/BBC_Radio_1#First_broadcast
[119] https://en.wikipedia.org/wiki/John_Entwistle
[120] *Penguin Pocket On This Day*. Penguin Reference Library. 2006. ISBN 978-0-14-102715-9.
[121] "Cumbernauld Town Centre". Retrieved 2012-08-08.
[122] Bullock, John (1993). *The Rootes Brothers: story of a motoring empire*. Sparkford: Patrick Stephens Ltd. ISBN 978-1-85260-454-7.
[123] "1967: Queen Elizabeth 2 takes to the waves". *BBC News*. 20 September 1967. Archived from the original on 30 January 2008. Retrieved 2008-02-03.
[124] "Historic Background" (PDF). Northamptonshire County Council. Retrieved 2011-08-12.
[125] "The closing of Baggeridge Colliery". Black Country Society. Archived from the original on 19 July 2011. Retrieved 2011-08-12.
[126] BBC On This Day [3] 1968: Surgeons conduct UK's first heart transplant
[127] Palmer, Alan; Veronica (1992). *The Chronology of British History*. London: Century Ltd. pp. 427-428. ISBN 978-0-7126-5616-0.
[128] "Newcastle United 3 Man City 4". *Football-england.com*. Retrieved 2011-08-12.
[129] "1968: Manchester United win European Cup". *BBC News*. 29 May 1968. Archived from the original on 21 January 2008. Retrieved 2008-01-15.
[130] "1968: Alec Rose sails home". *BBC News*. 4 July 1968. Archived from the original on 19 December 2007. Retrieved 2008-01-15.
[131] *Vocal Selections: Joseph and the Amazing Technicolor Dreamcoat*. Milwaukee, WI: Hal Leonard. 1994. ISBN 978-0 -7935-3427-2.
[132] "About The Show". The Really Useful Group. Archived from the original on 25 December 2008. Retrieved 2008-12-29.
[133] "Joseph and the Amazing Technicolor Dreamcoat". *AndrewLloyd Webber.com*. 1991. Archived from the original on 23 October 2010. Retrieved 2010-10-08.
[134] "1968: Musical Hair open as censors withdraw".*BBC News*. 27 September 1968. Retrieved 2008-01-15.
[135] Marr, Andrew (2007). *A History of Modern Britain*. London: Macmillan. p.281. ISBN 978-1-4050-0538-8.
[136] https://en.wikipedia.org/wiki/1968_in_British_music
[137] https://en.wikipedia.org/wiki/Bill_Medley
[138] https://en.wikipedia.org/wiki/Sandie_Shaw

[139] *Penguin Pocket On This Day*. Penguin Reference Library. 2006. ISBN 978-0-14-102715-9.
[140] Motorways – West Yorkshire
[141] http://en.wikipedia.org/wiki/1968_in_the_United_Kingdom
[142] 'Andy' (2 September 2006). "1968 and 1969: The Space Hopper in Britain". *Spacehopper*. Retrieved 2010-09-09.
[143] "Haweswater". RSPB. Retrieved 2007-04-04.
[144] "1969: Matt Busby retires from Man United". *BBC News*. 14 January 1969. Archived from the original on 17 January 2008. Retrieved 2008-01-10.
[145] "1969: Manchester City". *The FA Cup*. Retrieved 2011-11-12.
[146] "28 April 1969-Liverpool 0 Leeds United 0". *The Mighty Mighty Whites: the definitive history of Leeds United*. Retrieved 2011-11-12.
[147] *Penguin Pocket On This Day*. Penguin Reference Library. 2006. ISBN 0-14-102715-0.
[148] "1969: Lulu ties knot with Bee Gee". *BBC News*. 18 February 1969. Archived from the original on 1 January 2008. Retrieved 2008-01-10.
[149] http://en.wikipedia.org/wiki/1969_in_the_United_Kingdom
[150] Revoir, Paul (7 October 2008). "The most watched TV shows of all time – and they are all old programmes". *Daily Mail*. Retrieved 2011-03-03.
[151] "June anniversaries". *The BBC Story*. BBC. Archived from the original on 28 January 2011. Retrieved 2011-03-03.
[152] Palmer, Alan; Veronica (1992). *The Chronology of British History*. London: Century Ltd. pp. 429-430. ISBN 0-7126-5616-2.
[153] "Colour Television Chronology". *British TV History*. Archived from the original on 27 October 2010. Retrieved 2010-10-05.
[154] "On Her Majesty's Secret Service (1969)". *MI6*. Retrieved 2010-10-05.
[155] https://en.wikipedia.org/wiki/1969_in_British_Music
[156] https://en.wikipedia.org/wiki/Kiki_Dee
[157] "1969: Murdoch wins Fleet Street foothold". *BBC News*. 2 January 1969. Archived from the original on 7 March 2008. Retrieved 2008-02-11.
[158] "B&Q Online: From Kitchens & Bathrooms to Sheds & Paving; plus planning tools". Retrieved 23 January 2011.
[159] Sawyer, Miranda (17 July 2004). "Fear of diy-ing". *The Guardian* (London). Retrieved 2010-04-26.
[160] "1969: New 50-pence coin sparks confusion". *BBC News*. 14 October 1969. Retrieved 2008-01-10.
[161] "Ford Capri Mk 1 and Mk 1 Facelift". *Retro Car Icons*. Retrieved 2014-03-03.
[162] *AROnline*

Printed in Great Britain
by Amazon